Communicating can help you to be smarter, happier, better-looking, and improve your quality of life.

BE SMARTER, HAPPIER, BETTER-LOOKING.

How communicating can improve your quality of life

BRENT NELSON PH. D.

HH

Heather Hill

Cover Art BNelson

Copyright © 2016 - All Rights Reserved
ISBN 10:069255940X- ISBN 13:978-0692559406

Table of Contents

Preface

Every day you make decisions and face problems that need to be solved. You might feel that you should be making better decisions and finding better solutions to your problems. But, you may not know what to do.

You may feel your relationships aren't as good as they should be. You may want to have supportive relationships with your family and friends. You might feel that you should be getting along better with your partner, spouse, or children. But you aren't sure where to begin.

You may feel that you should be doing better at work. You would like to get along better with your coworkers and boss. You might be part of a group that's not getting things done. And you don't know why.

You might feel uneasy when faced with a conflict or crisis. Things in the past could have gone better, and you might think about what you could have done different.

You might wish that you felt better about yourself or looked better. You may think that you should feel better about what you've accomplished. But don't know where things went wrong.

If you feel this way you are not alone.

All too often we feel frustrated with our life. We may feel bad about things, but don't know why. We might wish we could do better, but don't know what to do.

This book was written to help you. While a book can't solve your problems, it can help to increase your awareness so you can better understand why you feel the way you do. It can provide you with options, so you can do something about it.

However, only you can determine what is best for you. By increasing your awareness and having more options you can begin to feel better and be smarter, happier, and even better-looking.

In conducting seminars, speaking, and teaching graduate and undergraduate classes, more and more people kept asking if there was a practical guide to help them communicate better at work and at home.

This book utilizes scholarly research in new and creative ways for the purpose of reporting, commentary, analysis, and criticism to create new knowledge and insights. It is written in a casual, conversational style for ease of reading with minimal technical terms. This book can be used in courses, seminars, or as a resource for schools, businesses, groups, and organizations.

This book uses the words "communicating" or "communicate" instead of "communication" because communicating is an active process between people rather than communication, which can seem more passive or technical.

**Communicating begins with one person
and as the reader of this book that person is you.**

Communicating is important because of the amount of time we spend communicating.

* It is how we gain information and new ideas.
* It is how we learn to do things.
* It is how we develop our identity and self-concept.
* It is how we can help our career and promote personal growth.
* It is how we support others and show that we care about them.
* It is how we create and maintain relationships.
* It is how we get to know ourselves, others, and the world around us.

This book does not advocate a specific course of action. There is no best "one size fits all" approach that works for everyone all of the time. It is not meant to provide legal, financial, psychological, relationship, or other types of professional advice.

This book utilizes naturalistic observation as a research methodology through observation and participation in the natural environment. This is similar to how we learn much of what we know. Naturalistic observation, interviews, focus groups, seminars, and experience provided the basis of the knowledge utilized herein.

The author of this book is the first person to develop and apply new and innovative methodologies to understand how people are motivated by laws that govern communicating and behavior. The author of this book is the first person to identify these laws, the *Nelsonian Laws of Uncertainty, Shared meaning, and Investing*, which comprise a *Grand Unified Theory of Behavioral Communication*. These laws have influenced people's behavior since the beginning of time.

This book describes how uncertainty affects us and influences our lives, including how we communicate and our behavior. It can help to increase your awareness of how uncertainty affects you. It can provide options about how to communicate more effectively to improve your quality of life. It can even help you to be smarter, happier, and better-looking,

Chapter 1
Be Smarter and Happier by Communicating

How do you know what you know? How do you know what is true? In the past people developed knowledge they believed to be true, which we now know is not.

Consider that, a second century astronomer determined that the sun and all the planets revolved around the earth. In medieval times, it was thought that alchemy could turn lead into gold. In colonial times, some women were thought to be witches. More recently, it was thought that cigarettes had health benefits because they were both a stimulant and relaxant.

So, how do we know that what we believe today is true? How do we know it won't be proven false in the future? Some societies thought that human sacrifices or the burning of witches was right. So, what are we doing today that we consider right because some people perceive it's right, but may not be in the future?

If enough people decide something is right, does that make it right?

How do we come to know what we know? We all have our own ways of obtaining information to know what we know. Much of what we know we learn through our education and experiences. This can make it difficult to change what people already know because they may resist new information, perhaps even becoming defensive.

When we want to know something how do we find out about it?
- We might ask others who have experience.
- We might look to the past to see how it was done before.
- We might look for inspiration through spiritual revelation.
- We might look at what we know in the present using methods like trial and error.
- We might look to the scientific method to create new knowledge in the future.

We create knowledge in the following ways to understand the world around us.
- Perceiving. Gaining knowledge through our five senses; sight, sound, touch, taste, and smell.
- Doing. Gaining knowledge through experience by participating.
- Thinking. Gaining knowledge through education, rationality, logic, or scientific inquiry.
- Believing. Gaining knowledge through religion or faith by trusting in something unseen.
- Realizing. Gaining knowledge through instinct or revelation.
- Feeling. Gaining knowledge through intuition, emotions, or empathy.

Knowledge is not just about how we gain information, it's also about how we use it. Gaining new knowledge works like the perception process where we select, organize, and interpret information to give it meaning, so it fits in with what we already know. When we feel uncertainty, we are more likely to be open to new knowledge. When someone is overly certain, they are not necessarily open to new ideas.

Throughout history, many people were certain about things they believed to be true, which sometimes resulted in disastrous consequences.

People may resist changing what they believe to be true. Rather than trying to convince them to change what they know, challenge them to think beyond what they know. People are less likely to want to be perceived as being unwilling to learn something new. Ask them if they feel that they already know everything there is to know, so they don't need to learn anything new.

The Process of Communicating

The process of communicating provides a way to understand how we communicate by looking at the individual elements in the process. It helps us to see how these elements work together so that we can be better understood by other people. We often communicate without thinking how things work, so when they don't go as we want, like when we are misunderstood, we may not know what to do.

How people communicate involves a number of elements that occur seamlessly so that we don't think much about them. It can be helpful to break the process down into its elements to help understand how it works. By understanding the process of communicating, you can develop skills to communicate more effectively with other people.

You, your desired outcome, your Great Idea, others, connections, The Great Abyss, feedback, and effectiveness are all elements in the process of communicating. Being aware of these elements and how they work provides a way to talk about how we communicate, so that we can communicate more effectively with others.

The process of communicating begins with you.

• You. You are the creator and communicator of your message, so the process of communicating begins with you. Since everyone is unique, you have your own unique way of doing things that includes your own style of communicating. Becoming more effective at communicating involves knowing your own individual style of communicating and being able to adapt your style to the situation, while still being yourself.

Some things that influence your style of communicating include your background, interests, and experiences. A person's first interactions are with their family, so this is where they first learn how to communicate with others. People may keep these ways of communicating throughout their life.

Desired Outcome

We communicate not only to share information, but also to get things done. We often determine what we want in terms of achieving goals and objectives, but desired outcome is different.

Goals and objectives can be specific things we want to achieve, so we develop a plan and pursue a course of action that can put us on a single path leaving little room for alternative ways to achieve them. By pursuing fixed goals and objectives we might miss opportunities that present themselves along the way.

Using sports as an example, a goal or objective can be making a goal, basket, home run, or touchdown to help win the game. It is a clear, definite action that is either accomplished or not. Since not every team can win every game, goals and objectives can be discouraging, even hurt our self-concept.

A desired outcome approach considers your general sense of well-being such as personal growth and development, working better as a team, and enjoyment of the game regardless of winning or losing. While losing a game will not accomplish your objective, you can still achieve your desired outcome.

Desired outcome is what you want to happen after others get your message.

Desired outcome is more general in nature and considers the big picture. It encourages you to consider more than one path to achieve what you want so you can select the most effective one and switch them as needed or if you run into difficulties. This enables you to pursue any opportunities you might find. Desired outcome focuses less on achieving specific goals or objectives and more on fulfilling your needs and wants, which provides more flexibility in how you fulfill them.

While your desired outcome is about what you want to happen after you communicate with others, rather than looking for something specific to happen, take a big picture approach focusing on your general state of well-being. This increases the number of ways to reach your desired outcome, so you have more flexibility.

Increased flexibility can improve your effectiveness by reducing the prospect of not achieving your desired outcome. If one approach doesn't work, you can switch to another. This helps to create a more positive climate to encourage others to work with you to achieve your desired outcome.

When you know your desired outcome, you can spend time on what really matters. Everyone has tasks to accomplish, but a desired outcome is more than that. Simply accomplishing tasks themselves may not achieve your desired outcome.

This can be why we might feel that we are working all the time, but not getting anywhere. This could be one reason seemingly successful people may be frustrated or unhappy, because they focus on accomplishing tasks or achieving goals and objectives, while neglecting their desired outcomes.

Focusing on achieving your desired outcome can be a more positive approach because it is less discouraging when what you want to happen does not happen. It helps avoid making judgments about things being good and bad or feeling like a failure. It allows you to find partial success in what you do because pursuing a desired outcome considers the big picture and your state of well-being.

• Unintended or Undesired Outcomes. There are times when we try to achieve our desired outcome and things don't go the way we would like them to go. This can create unintended or undesired outcomes. An unintended outcome is a result that we did not expect, it can be positive or negative or a little bit of both. We may have asked for a raise, but instead we were given a promotion or a pay cut.

An undesired outcome is when we get a result we do not want. We may want to get a raise, but end up being fired. We never wanted to be fired and if given a choice we would have stayed at the same salary. Because it is undesired, it is generally considered negative.

It can help to look at your desired outcome from the other person's point of view to consider how they might react. We often focus on what we want to happen rather than thinking about what others might do in response. No matter how effectively we communicate, there is always the possibility that instead of achieving our desired outcome we might get an undesired or unintended outcome.

Your Great Idea

Your Great Idea is the message you want to communicate. It is the part of the process of communicating that consists of the information you communicate to others. It begins with the message, which is what you say or write, but it can also consist of other elements like nonverbal information including facial expressions and gestures. It usually starts with an idea that exists in our mind not just in words, but also in pictures.

In order to communicate your Great Idea to other people, it has to be in a form that others can understand. This usually involves putting ideas into words that are spoken or written. The words and letters themselves are just symbols that have no inherent meaning. Meaning is given to them by the people who receive them.

When they receive the message, they translate the words back into ideas to understand them. We use shared meaning to go through this process of investing symbols with meaning and translating that meaning into ideas. We do this so often it happens naturally without much thought.

When we speak, our mind automatically translates our ideas into words and when we read or hear words they are automatically converted into ideas. This means that the meanings are in the minds of people and not necessarily in the symbols themselves.

For example, when you see the word TREE, you don't think oh, that's four letters. In your mind you see a picture of a big green plant with a trunk, branches, and leaves or needles. This is because everyone who understands English has learned that these four letters are symbols that represent a big green thing. The word TREE is not actually a living tree.

Using symbols is critical to communicating because if every time we wanted to communicate the idea of a tree, we would have to describe it or show one to others and that would take a lot of time. Instead, we take the symbols T R E E and invest them with meaning, so the letters become a shorthand reference that refers to the real big green thing.

• Others. In the process of communicating everything begins with you, so in this book, anyone else you communicate with whether it's just one person or a large number of people are referred to as "others." Other people have their own style of communicating and characteristics that give them their own personality. These characteristics can affect how they communicate with you. This can help or hinder the communicating process and how well your message comes across to them.

To communicate effectively, it is helpful to be aware of the unique communicating styles of others to help adapt your own communicating style to them, while still being you. The same things that influence your style of communicating like family, culture, education, religion, and geographic affiliation also influence how others communicate with you.

Everyone has different communicating skills, so it's helpful to be aware of their skills to help you to communicate more effectively with them. Sometimes a perceived unwillingness to communicate with you is not about you, but rather about the other person's comfort level with their communicating skills.

In order to effectively communicate with others, it's helpful to be aware of what things might affect why others communicate with you. They are more likely to communicate about things they are interested in or that they like. By having an awareness of how the process of communicating works and how it affects others, we can adapt our own style to communicate more effectively with them.

• Connections. Once you have created your Great Idea you need a connection to communicate with others. A connection is the means by which you communicate with others, so that they can receive your message. If there is no connection, they cannot get your message.

Some connections include speaking face to face, telephone calls, writing a letter or email, public speaking, or through the media. We can make connections with others through our five senses of sight, sound, touch, taste, and smell.

We all have different ways that we get information. When you use several connections, you increase the chance that people understand and remember your message. For example, if you want your children to be on time for dinner, you could use several connections using different senses.

You can tell them, leave a note on the refrigerator, and use food that smells good to attract their attention. On a romantic date we can make several connections with our date through our appearance, music, perfume or flowers, food, and touch. Increasing the number of connections can make an experience more intense.

The Great Abyss

You communicate your Great Idea by making a connection with others. Ideally they would receive and understand your message, however, things can get in the way. Making a connection does not necessarily mean they will understand you. There can be a huge chasm that separates you from them. In order to effectively communicate with others, you must make a connection to get your message across this chasm without it getting lost. This can be characterized as "The Great Abyss."

The Great Abyss can be thought of like a swamp or chasm that has to be crossed in order to make a connection with others. It characterizes everything that can potentially get in the way of you effectively communicating with others, so that they don't get your intended message. Instead, they may get a different idea, the wrong message, or nothing at all which could result in undesired or unintended outcomes.

These are some of the types of interference in The Great Abyss.

• External interference. This includes things that people hear in their physical surroundings that can interfere with your message. This can include things like an air conditioner, radio, television, traffic, or other people talking. This interference can mask or distract others from hearing and fully understanding your message.

• Internal interference. These are things that occur in people's minds that interfere with how they perceive your Great Idea. They may have a short attention span, their mind wanders, or they think about other things. Interference can also be physiological, they may be tired or not feeling well.

They may not understand your Great Idea because they may not have the same background, education, experience, or expectations as you. By being aware of potential sources of interference, you can communicate in ways that minimize their impact. Using repetition, emphasizing important points, and soliciting feedback can help to cut through this type of interference.

By knowing how The Great Abyss works, we can communicate more effectively with others to get and keep their attention. If people need or want something they are less likely to filter it out.

• Point of view. This is how people see things including themselves, others, and the world around them. Everyone has their own unique point of view which is often based upon their past experiences.

A point of view influences how people communicate with one another and affects what they pay attention to or ignore. It affects how they interpret and understand what you communicate to them. By being aware of other people's point of view, you can communicate more effectively with them.

• Frames of reference. A frame of reference is like the frame of a window or the viewfinder of a camera. It frames what a person can see or wants to see and everything outside the frame is blocked out or ignored. People can choose what things to let through their frames and what things to keep out.

This can also happen subconsciously, so people may not be aware that they are doing it. A person's frame of reference can be based upon their interests, education, and past experiences. By being aware of how frames of reference work, you can create messages to get through them.

• Preconceptions. People tend to block out information that is contrary to what they feel they already know. For instance, if they have one political point of view they may block out information from other points of view that contradict their own even if they know that the information is accurate. Because people tend to be more receptive to messages that fall within their preconceptions, it can be helpful to know what they are to shape your message to fit within them.

• Filters. Every day we are inundated with so many messages we block out many of them. These messages come from people around us or the media. We can receive more information then we need, so we filter some of it out. This is one reason why people generally tend to pay attention to only a small amount of information that is communicated to them. They pay attention to what they feel is important and filter out the rest.

• Attention span. The length of our attention span is contingent on many things like being tired, overworked, bored, or having too much information. For example, when we are driving we do not pay attention to all the signs we pass because we see so many. If we paid attention to all of them it would hinder our driving.

Have you ever been in a car with someone who felt the need to read every sign out loud as you pass? Was it helpful or annoying? That's what it would be like if we paid attention to everything that is communicated to us. However, if we are almost out of gas we pay attention to every sign looking for a gas station.

• Feedback. You have your Great Idea, made a connection, and crossed The Great Abyss to communicate with others. So, how do you know if they got your message? Feedback can help you find out if your Great Idea has been received.

Feedback can happen in several ways. It can happen informally by asking questions or having others restate your ideas to determine if they fully understand them. It can happen in formal ways like surveys, interviews, polls, or focus groups.

It is important that feedback be accurate and honest. A conversation is the best means of feedback because it is instantaneous. Other types of feedback like surveys and polls can be helpful, but may be less accurate.

• Effectiveness. Rather than thinking of how you communicate as being good or bad, think of communicating effectively. The more you understand others and the more they understand you, the more effectively you can communicate with them.

**Effective communicating is how well others receive
your Great Idea and if you achieve your desired outcome.**

Looking at how you communicate in terms of effectiveness, rather than good or bad, can help you to determine what works and what could be improved. It can give you a more realistic idea of your skills so that you can feel better about what you can do and work on developing what could be done better.

Styles of Communicating

When people create their Great Idea they may use a particular style of communicating to make a connection with others. In order to communicate more effectively, it is helpful to recognize these styles and be aware of their strengths and weaknesses. How people communicate with others can be characterized by three basic styles.

The first style, the arrow approach.

This style of communicating is similar to shooting an arrow into the air and hoping it hits the target. In this approach, a person creates their Great Idea, sends it to others through a connection, and then waits for the result. They hope it is received and understood. The people who receive it may not fully understand the message or may interpret it differently than it was intended.

While this sounds like it could create misunderstandings, it is how people have been communicating for a long time. Much of the news and information we receive that influences our perceptions and expectations is communicated through the media using this approach. In a business, the CEO often sends orders down each level of management telling employees what to do. This style lacks an effective means to provide feedback to know if their message was understood.

The second style, the tennis approach.

This second style of communicating resolves some of the problems with the first style. People needed to know if their Great Idea was accurately received, so a way to get feedback from those receiving the message was added. This approach encourages the person receiving the message to communicate back to the person who sent it to determine how well it was understood. The original sender could then decide if additional information needs to be sent to clarify it.

This approach works like a game of tennis where one person creates their Great Idea and then hits it over the net hoping the other person will get it. If the other person returns the ball it's a success. We use this style when we send emails, memos, and phone messages. This style offers some improvement over the first method because there is a mechanism to provide feedback to clarify the original message. It is commonly used even though it can be confusing and time consuming.

The third style, the conversational approach.

This style of communicating fixes many of the problems of the first and second styles. It is more realistic and effective because it is like having a conversation where people both speak and listen as well as provide information and ask questions. It is the most effective approach, but it can take the most energy. It is often preferred because it takes into account the individuals involved and the context of the situation.

The conversational approach is a collaborative process where people work together to achieve a common understanding. This style works well in situations where instantaneous feedback will help the process. For example, if you are trying to fix a computer it can be difficult reading a manual and could take forever to get the information you need using email. Having a conversation provides direct feedback to make the process easier.

We use this style when we see someone face to face and have a conversation or when we speak to them over the telephone. A short conversation can accomplish more than dozens of emails because we can communicate exactly what we want, clarify information, and ask or answer questions more quickly. However, people may avoid it, using the other two styles by texting and emailing because they can be reviewed and edited before sending. They may feel conversation is too spontaneous or risky increasing their anxiety and uncertainty, so they avoid it.

In order to communicate more effectively, it is helpful to recognize when to use each of these styles of communicating and why. While the third style is the most effective, consider just how often people use the first two. We use the first two styles because they can be easier and quicker saving us time. Each of these styles can be useful depending on your desired outcome, so it can be helpful to be aware of their limitations.

Chapter 2
Be Smarter Creating Your Message

Before you can communicate your Great Idea to others you first need to create it. You might want to give a presentation, write a report, or make a video. While these situations are different, the process of creating them has similar elements.

Instead of describing each of these separately, the following process can be used to create your message to use in many different situations. This process provides options so you can choose what works best for you in your own situation.

The process of creating a message
to communicate with others begins with you.

To communicate effectively with other people, it's helpful to know yourself including your communicating skills, background, experiences, credibility, and competence. It can be helpful to reduce uncertainty for your audience by letting them know something about yourself through the appropriate use of self-disclosure.

You might tell them about yourself, your experiences, accomplishments, and expertise to communicate confidence and credibility, so the audience will be more receptive to you.

In most forms of public communicating, your Great Idea needs to be written down before being put in its final form. The old adage to begin at the beginning is not necessarily the most effective way to get started. Getting your Great Idea down on paper can be difficult, so don't get bogged down with what to write first.

Start with what is important, interesting, or what you know the most about, then fill in the rest later. You are creating a message for a reason, so start with that first.

Consider these options when creating your Great Idea.

• Uncertainty. When you communicate in public there is often a high degree of uncertainty in your audience about you and your Great Idea. Look for ways to reduce uncertainty to make your audience more receptive to your message. This can be done by providing relevant information about yourself and your message.

• Share meaning. Look for ways to connect to your audience by sharing meaning through appropriate self-disclosure like telling stories about yourself and your experiences.

• Invest. Encourage your audience to invest in your Great Idea by providing information that can be useful or beneficial to them.

• Desired outcome. To create an effective message it's helpful to determine your desired outcome. Your desired outcome is more than just a goal or objective, it is what you want your audience to think or do after they receive your message. In determining your desired outcome it is helpful to have realistic expectations about your audience and what they can do because unrealistic expectations can lead to frustration or disappointment.

• The topic. What one or two things should your audience remember even if they forget everything else about your message? Asking this should give you your topic.

Your topic is the subject of your message, your main idea, thesis, or claim. A good topic is something that interests you as well as your audience. Keep it simple and straightforward. You should be able to summarize your topic in a single sentence.

• The claim. If you're making a critical argument, the topic is referred to as the claim. You support your claim using evidence put together with logic and reasoning. All the information in your message should support your claim. Information is structured using reasoning to make it persuasive to the audience. A claim is often used in more formal methods of communicating. For example, an attorney in court makes a claim of guilt or innocence that is supported with evidence.

• Scope. Consider the scope of your message including its depth and breadth. The breadth is how much information you cover and the depth is how specific or detailed you get. The combination you choose depends on your message and your audience. In order to determine this consider the knowledge of your audience, your knowledge, and the time that is available. It's better to cover less information and have your audience understand your message than to try to do too much.

Your Audience

**It is helpful to know as much about your audience
as you can to make a connection with them.**

People are more likely to be open to information that they find useful, interesting, entertaining, or is in their best interest.
• By knowing how they form their perceptions, you can develop a message that cuts through the interference to get across The Great Abyss.
• By knowing their expectations, you can create your message to meet them.
• By knowing their needs and wants, you can focus your message to better fulfill them.
• By knowing their desired outcomes, you can target your message to help them to achieve them.

There are several ways to get to know your audience. If you are speaking to a group, talk to people as they are arriving and get to know them. For larger audiences interviews, focus groups, and surveys can be used to learn about their interests.

Be aware of these audience characteristics when creating your message.

• Audience needs and wants. People pay attention to information that will help them fulfill their needs and wants. The more you know what these are, the more likely they are to pay attention to you. If they are looking for information to help them fulfill their needs and wants, they are more likely to be open to your message.

• Audience perceptions. Be aware of your audience's perception of you and your message. You can use identity management and appropriate self-disclosure to make them more receptive to your message. Present information that is similar to their perceptions and expectations to make it easier for your message to fit in with what they already know. Be aware of the perceptions they have of themselves and know if their perceptions accurately reflect reality or not.

• Audience expectations. People have expectations of you and your message. Be aware of them, so you can meet them as reasonably as possible. They also have expectations about themselves and just how much they are willing to do. So, be realistic in what you expect them to do because they are only able to do so much.

• Audience types. There are two types of audiences. The first is your primary audience. This is the audience that will receive your message. The other is your secondary audience. These are the people who might receive your message through other connections. Either one or both can be your target audience. For example, a political candidate may speak at a convention, which is their primary audience. Their secondary audience is people who were not there, but may see it on television, hear it on the radio, or read about the speech in print or the internet.

• Demographics. These are traits people have that can be observed or rather easily identified. They include age, gender, ethnicity, geographic affiliation, group affiliation, education, or economic status. Audience research is often based upon demographics to help understand the behavior of groups of people. By having an awareness of your audience's demographics, you can structure your message to reach them more effectively.

• Psychographics. These are traits that are unique to each person like their interests, hobbies, likes, dislikes, behaviors, and psychological makeup. These provide information about an audience's needs and wants, behavior, motivation, and desired outcomes. They can help you to create a message that makes a connection to cut through the interference of The Great Abyss to reach them and help you to achieve your desired outcome.

• Group affiliation. It's helpful to know what groups your audience belongs to because group members often share common interests and groups exert a degree of influence over their members. Utilizing information that is of interest to group members can reduce uncertainty to make them more receptive to your message, so you can achieve your desired outcome.

• Knowledge. It's helpful to know what knowledge your audience has about your topic to determine how much background information to cover, so they will understand your message. You want to avoid covering information they already know because they might find it boring.

• Don't include information they don't understand. For instance, your message would be different if you were speaking to a professional group or the general public. If you are unsure of their level of knowledge, take a middle of the road approach by not being too specific or too general. Clearly define any terms or concepts you use.

• The context. All communication takes place within a context or situation. It can be helpful to know as much as possible about what is happening that could affect how people perceive your message. This can include people's past experiences and future expectations.

Levels of Response

The following levels of response looks at communicating from the audience's perspective by considering what their potential response might be. Each level represents increased acceptance of your message. These levels can affect their behavior and how they communicate with you. It starts with the most basic and easy to achieve going to the most advanced and difficult.

Level I. Awareness. This is the most basic level of response. The purpose is to increase your audience's knowledge and understanding of your subject. It is the easiest response to achieve because the audience does not have to do anything more than listen to you and understand your message. Awareness includes informing, defining, explaining, or demonstrating something to make it more familiar to your audience.

Level II. Agreement. When people agree with us, it makes us feel good about ourselves. Agreeing on issues that are part of our values and beliefs can be more difficult because it involves information that may be contrary to our self-concept or social reality. The more something involves our self-concept or view of social reality, the more difficult it can be to change because it may create uncertainty. So, if you are looking for agreement have realistic expectations.

Level III. Action. This level involves motivating people to do something you want them to do. There can be many kinds of action from buying a product or supporting a cause, to changing their lifestyle. This can also include getting people to stop doing something, like smoking. This level includes the other two because in order for them to take action, they must be informed and agree with your idea. Then you can use persuasion to motivate them to take action. Getting your audience to take action is more difficult because they have to do more than just think about it.

Methods that motivate people to take action are often based on uncertainty because it is uncomfortable and people don't like being uncomfortable. Uncertainty can create emotions like anxiety, fear, or anger. While it may seem like a good idea to use positive emotions to motivate people, if the emotion is positive there is little discomfort.

Negative emotions can be powerful motivators because they can increase a person's level of discomfort and uncertainty. When people feel enough discomfort they are more likely to be motivated to do something about it. The more intense the emotion and the more uncomfortable it makes them, the more motivated they become.

When people want others to do something, they might try to make them angry or fearful because emotions are a powerful motivator.

If you want to motivate people to take action, consider what kind of action you want them to take. Do you want them to take action before, during, or after something happens? These are three options.

- Proactive. Taking action before something happens by getting ahead of the curve like with preventative medicine.
- Interactive. Taking action while something is happening by riding the curve like treating an illness.
- Reactive. Taking action after something happens by following the curve like finding a cure.

Level IV. Actuation. This is the most difficult level of response because it involves the most change. It not only involves people agreeing with an idea and taking action, but also spreading the word to inform and persuade others about it. This makes it the least likely outcome because it involves adopting a belief, motivating behavior, and sharing it with others. Actuation is often used in social, political, environmental, and religious causes. For example, people may agree with and support a political candidate, and then go out to campaign for them as well.

Persuasion

The second, third, and fourth levels of response share the common element of persuasion. We use persuasion to get others to agree with us or to motivate their behavior. These are options that are effective in persuading others.

• Reasoning. We persuade others by using forms of evidence organized by reasoning that build an argument to achieve our desired outcome. Our desired outcome can be called the premise, thesis, or claim. We support a claim of evidence based upon established standards and criteria rationally organized to reach a conclusion. This method is persuasive because it is presented as objective and logical instead of being subjective and open to opinion.

• Emotions. Emotions appeal to our values and beliefs. Common emotions include empathy, sadness, guilt, anger, or fear. Many emotions can be uncomfortable motivating us to take action. Emotional appeals are a powerful motivating force that can be used when reasoning may not be as effective or there is not sufficient evidence.

• Tradition. Traditions and rituals are an important part of who we are. They are part of our history and how we make connections with others. We celebrate important events by doing things that have been done by other people before us. Upholding traditions can be a powerful motivating force to persuade people because it represents stability and predictability.

• Authority. People can be persuaded based on the advice of a person who is considered an authority or has expertise, experience, credibility, or trustworthiness. We can be persuaded by people whose values we share or who we hold in high esteem. We can also be persuaded by well known personalities with whom we may feel a connection.

• Shared values. It's easier to persuade others when we have something in common with them like similar values or interests. Shared values form connections between people that can make them feel like we are all in this together. It's helpful to find some common ground between you and your audience because it makes them more likely to agree with you or to do what you want them to do.

• Needs and wants. People are always looking to fulfill needs and wants, so you can persuade them by providing something they need or want. By knowing your audience, you can tailor your message to include potential benefits for them. If they see that your message has something that will benefit or help them, they can be more likely to agree or take action.

Gathering Information

Once you have determined your desired outcome and developed your Great Idea, you will need to gather information. Information can come from a variety of sources and the best place to begin is with what you already know from your own experiences, education, and expertise. We gather information through observation, participation, and by learning from other people's knowledge and experience.

It can be helpful to be aware of these types of information.

• Primary sources. This is the best place to get information because it comes directly from the source, so it is the most current and accurate. These sources are usually individuals relating their own experiences and observations. They can also include research like interviews, statistics, and studies. This information can be the most difficult and time consuming to obtain, which is why we are more likely to use secondary sources.

• Secondary. This is information that comes from the original source through an intermediary like a reporter who interviews someone and then reports what they said. This means that the information can potentially be altered, edited, or changed. An intermediary can add their own views potentially changing its meaning. Secondary information is easier to obtain as it is more widely available.

• Quantitative and qualitative information. Quantitative information pertains to quantities, those things that can be measured or expressed by numbers like statistics. Statistics use numbers to measure things or represent information, so it can be used for analysis or comparison. This can make difficult information easier to understand. Qualitative information expresses the unique qualities of something that cannot be easily characterized by numbers, but rather by description, illustration, explanation, or narrative.

• Statistics. Some types of information can be presented in numerical form to make it easier to understand. Statistics and poll data is based on asking people questions, but their answers may not be truthful or accurate. Statistics can be manipulated based upon the questions you ask and who you ask. If you use statistics it's helpful to be sure the information is relevant to the topic, easy to understand, current, and from a credible source.

• Quotes are the words that someone has written or said. When the quote is from an expert or well known person, it can be used to support an argument by providing evidence. It's important that the quotes are accurate and relevant to the topic.

• Opinions are what people think about a topic. This can be an expert opinion, public opinion, or an average person's opinion. An expert can provide an opinion to support a claim whereas an average person can provide an opinion to illustrate public perception.

• Descriptions are based upon sensory information that creates a picture in the minds of the audience. You can use imagery to include impressions based on our five senses of sight, sound, taste, touch, and smell.

• Narratives provide information in the form of a story. We often express information about our past experiences and about people we know in narrative form.

• Illustrations provide an example by telling a story that can be either real or hypothetical.

• Explanations can tell us why something happened, its cause and effect, or how something came into being.

• Comparison and contrast uses two things to illustrate their differences or similarities. Contrast works by highlighting the differences between two things whereas comparison works by highlighting their similarities.

• Definitions take words or concepts that are unfamiliar to an audience and puts them in a familiar language.

• Examples are specific instances that can be real or hypothetical about a specific situation that has either happened or might happen.

Communicating an effective message depends on having quality information, so it is important to evaluate the information you use including its accuracy and validity. It should be relevant to your topic or support your claim. It should be current and accurate. It should come from credible sources like a recognized expert or authority. And it should be credible, trustworthy, and used accurately.

Gathering information for your message is like gathering evidence for a court case. In court, you want to prove your claim before a judge or jury who is hearing your case for the first time. So, how do you make your case? You provide evidence that is clear, accurate, easy to understand, and comes from credible sources.

The evidence is put together in an organized way that is easy to understand. Reasoning is used to explain how the evidence fits together to support your claim. It is helpful to be aware of any counter arguments that could undermine your claim and be ready to refute them.

Structure

Structure is how you organize and present your Great Idea to others. It includes methods of organization, use of evidence, and reasoning. It includes the major structural elements of your message including the introduction, main points, transitions, and conclusion. It includes how you use language, word choice, sentence structure, and paragraph organization. All these elements are arranged to make the message as effective as possible.

Once you have gathered the information you need, it has to be organized in a way that is easily understood by your audience. Organization deals with the perception process and the mind's ability to select, organize, and retain information. Most of the information we perceive is chaotic, received in random bits and pieces. Our mind organizes information by giving it structure, so that we can better understand it now and utilize it in the future.

You can make it easier for others to understand your Great Idea by utilizing these established methods of organization.

• Chronological. Ordering events as they happen in real time.
• Sequential. Presenting events in the order in which they need to happen like performing a task.
• Spatial. Describing how things are physically related to one another, like driving directions.

- Topical. This method organizes things by using standard topics or subjects.
- Numerical. This method ranks information based on a sequence of numbers or what things come first, second, last.
- Classification. This method organizes things by natural groups. Plants and animals are categorized by family and species based upon how they are related to one another.
- Cause and effect. This explains why something exists or how it came to be.
- Problem and solution. This method presents a problem that needs to be resolved and the solutions to resolve it.
- Need satisfaction. A need that must be fulfilled is established and then methods are suggested to fulfill that need.
- Importance. Items are organized in order of importance starting either with the least important to most important or the most important to the least.
- General to specific. Items are organized starting with the most general to the most specific or from the specific to the general.
- Comparison and contrast. Comparison is taking two things and relating their similarities. Contrast is taking two things and relating their differences.
- Complexity. This approach takes a concept or process from the simple to the difficult or the difficult to the simple. For example, learning to play the piano begins with simple music then moves to more difficult music.
- Structure. This approach takes something that is made up of smaller elements and describes how those elements fit together. For example, showing how a house is built by describing how each section is put together.
- Function. This approach looks at how things work or how they are utilized. For example, describing the human body might feature the circulatory or respiratory systems.
- Medical. Organizing approaches to problems like diagnosing an illness by identifying symptoms and prescribing treatments.
- The unknown. When communicating about something that an audience doesn't know about, begin with what they do know then connect it with what they don't know.
- Directions. This includes describing how to get somewhere, how to do something, or how something works. Describe the big picture so they know how everything fits together. Let them know where to begin and what things should look like at the end. Clarify the terms you use and be consistent using them. Use visual information to help them understand what you describe.

Outlines.

Before setting out to write your Great Idea it's helpful to make an outline. A good outline helps you to organize your ideas and clarify details, while looking at the big picture. There are basically two types of outlines.

The first is to help you construct your message. It is basically a list of your ideas organized in the order they will be presented. An outline makes it easier to make changes and move things around before you write them out. You can try different options to see which one works the best because once it's fully written out, it's more difficult to change.

The second type of outline can be used like a script when speaking or giving a presentation. The purpose of this outline is to help you stay on track, so you do not miss any information. It can be typed in a large easy to read font, so that words are not crowded together making it easy to follow. Number each page and perhaps even each line to help you keep track of where you are in case you lose your spot.

This type of outline can consist of the entire text, short sentences, keywords, or whatever combination works best for you. Some outlines are written in full text. For instance, when politicians give a speech they are likely to read the full text word for word off of a teleprompter. This is so they do not make any mistakes.

You can use a full sentence outline to keep on track or just keywords to cover basic ideas. Each has its own advantages and disadvantages. The more of your message that is written down, the more likely you are to sound like you are reading it.

However, this gives you the security of having all the information in front of you in case you need it. Using short statements or keywords helps you to sound more natural. However, there's less information to help you if you forget your lines or lose your place. If you are new to public speaking use full text outlines until you become comfortable speaking in public before using other types of outlines.

Writing delivery queues on an outline can help you communicate more effectively when giving a presentation or speaking to an audience. Delivery queues work like musical notation or stage directions in a script. You add words to your outline to tell you when to use vocal variety and nonverbal behavior, like gestures.

Vocal variety is how you say the words you speak including pacing, pauses, volume, intonation, and the pitch of your voice. Delivery queues can include nonverbal movements like gestures, facial expressions, moving about, and body language. Be sure to make these queues look different so you do not say them out loud. For example, to begin your speech you might write, "Good evening, (look at audience and smile)." This reminds you what to say and how to say it.

Introduction.

The first element of a message is the introduction. It can serve many purposes to give you options, so you can use one or a combination of the following approaches.

•   The introduction gets your audience's attention. You can begin by talking about current events, something relevant to your audience, the occasion, why everyone is gathered, something unusual or out of the ordinary, a humorous story, or a problem you propose to solve.

- The introduction reduces uncertainty about you and your message. It shapes your audience's perception of your message. Briefly outline your message, let them know your point of view, and what to expect so that they can follow you more easily.
- The introduction shares meaning to create a connection between you and the audience. Use a greeting or reference about something they are familiar with or interested in.
- The introduction encourages your audience to invest their time and attention in you and your message. Share some information about yourself, your interests, or an experience that you might have in common with your audience to motivate them to listen.
- The introduction creates the appropriate tone. You might use a funny anecdote, a serious illustration, or quote from someone who is well known.
- The introduction creates interest. Make your audience curious about what you have to say. Create a mystery that you will solve so they want to pay attention.

In order to share your Great Idea with others you have to cross The Great Abyss, which consists of all the things that get in the way of others receiving your message. It can include interference, other messages, or past experiences. People tend to look for things that fit in with their frames of reference, what they already know, or are familiar with because these reduce uncertainty.

Your audience can be influenced by their attitudes, opinions, or point of view. They are more likely to filter out information they think they don't need or does not interest them. There may also be background or psychological noise to distract them.

To effectively communicate your message, it should be presented in a way that overcomes this interference. The interference of The Great Abyss can be overcome by getting your audience's attention, generating interest, or showing how your message will benefit them. This should help to make them more receptive to your message, so they won't filter it out.

In a video, start with a wide angle shot to establish the scene, then go to close ups to show detail.

Start with the general and go to the specific.
Give them the big picture first, so they know where each part fits in.

These are some options to cut through the interference of The Great Abyss.

• Reduce uncertainty. People are interested in information that reduces uncertainty that makes them feel more comfortable, safe, and secure. They care about things they know about, that they feel close to, that they are comfortable with, or that are familiar to them. They want to know about things that happen close to them in their community, fits their interests, or that might affect them.

• Share Meaning. People are interested in information that shares meaning to make their experiences more interesting or significant. They are interested in things that they find unique, unusual, interesting, or out of the ordinary.

• Invest. People are interested in information they perceive as having value or that is important to them. They are interested in things they perceive might affect them now or in the future. They are interested in information that will benefit them or that they find useful.

• Needs and wants. People are interested in things that fulfill their needs and wants. They are interested in things that are new and relevant. They are interested in things that give them a sense of adventure or excitement. They are interested in things they find entertaining, exciting, humorous, suspenseful, or dramatic. They are interested in things that will increase their status, prestige, or bolster their self-concept.

Main points.

The main points of your message are the key ideas that support your claim or topic. You should be able to summarize each of these in a few words or a sentence. Your main points divide your message into several smaller ideas making them easier to organize.

It is helpful to focus your message by using as few main points as you need to communicate your message. Keep them consistent and relate them to one another, so your audience can follow them.

For each of your main points, give your audience the big picture first and then go into detail. This lets the audience know how everything fits together, so when you go into detail they will know where it fits in. Each main point is like a short message with a beginning and end.

A main point begins with a key idea followed by evidence to support it accompanied by an explanation, illustration, or example. Keep main points flexible so you can add or remove information if you need to change the length of your message.

Transitions.

Transitions are the links between sections of your message including the introduction, main points, and conclusion. Using transitions helps your message flow smoothly from one point to the next. They help structure and organize your ideas making them easier for your audience to understand.

Transitions can include a summary of the previous section or a preview of what's next. They may provide directions like describing a process. They can provide guidelines for the audience like chronological, numerical, or spatial references.

In a video, transitions are the edits between shots and are generally cuts, fades, or wipes. They set the tone, pacing, and emotional intensity. Transitions between scenes help the audience follow the story.

These are options for transitions.

- Time transitions use chronological relationships and words like now, then, before, after, sooner, later, or meanwhile.
- Connective transitions bridge ideas using words like and, also, moreover, in addition, however, but, instead, or although.
- Sequential transitions follow numerical patterns like first, second, third, last.
- Illustrative transitions set out ideas to illustrate points by using words like for example, for instance, or to illustrate.
- Inclusive transitions wrap up ideas by using words like to conclude, to summarize, therefore, as a result, or consequently.

Conclusion.

The conclusion is how you end your message. It wraps everything up, but is more than simply restating what's already been said. It's like the end of a movie, where everything is resolved for the audience. It can provide a reward to the audience for investing their time and paying attention to your message.

The conclusion can be as simple as thanking them for their time or it could provide valuable information that is useful to them. There are many types of conclusions and many are similar to introductions. You can use a quote, illustration, story, example, personal experience, surprise, or challenge them to do something.

The conclusion should wrap up everything and answer any questions the audience might have. It can be used for emotional effect much like music uses a crescendo where the emotional level builds to the end. You could use a decrescendo where the emotional level tapers off to a quiet ending.

The conclusion should include the one or two ideas that you want the audience to remember, not just after you finish, but much later. This is your last opportunity to get your point across, so let them know what you want them to remember.

Style.

Whether they are spoken or written, almost all messages involve some writing, which means there is a style of writing. Writing style includes the tone, mood, point of view, and structure of your message. The tone can range from serious to sad to sentimental to humorous. The mood can range from somber to happy.

• Point of view can range from your own, to others, to third person. The style you choose is based upon your desired outcome, your experience, your topic, or your audience. Styles can range from formal to informal, structured to conversational.

• Mood and tone. The mood sets the emotional feeling of a message. It can be warm and friendly, serious and somber, or scary and threatening. The tone is the general quality or tenor of the message. This is determined based upon you and your audience's attitude toward the topic.

• Emotional intensity. In creating a message, think about what emotions may be most effective in achieving your desired outcome. These can include happy, sad, sentimental, humorous, fearful, or angry. Emotions can be used as a means of persuasion or to gain people's attention. Emotions can have degrees of intensity. For example, movies often increase in emotional intensity as the plot progresses to keep the audience interested and build suspense.

• Pacing. The rate at which information is presented to an audience can range from fast to slow. If the pacing is too fast there can be information overload and people can become confused. If the pace is too slow people might get bored. Fast pacing can present more information in a shorter amount of time making things sound dramatic or exciting. Slow pacing can help people to better understand the message. Changes in pacing can draw out important information and be used for dramatic effect.

• Language. The kind of language we use depends on our message, topic, desired outcome, and the audience. How we use it can influence how others perceive us. Through the kind of language we use we can communicate information about ourselves including our expertise, credibility, confidence, and competence. Avoid clichés, slang, and technical jargon that people may not understand.

Talk about things as if they are happening in the present rather than the past to make them more interesting. Use descriptive language to help the audience visualize what you're talking about by creating a picture in their mind. Repeating words or phrases creates a rhythm that can give speech a musical or poetic quality.

Language can be artistic, emotional, and inspiring.

• Creativity. Creativity comes from your unique outlook, experiences, and characteristics. It can be developed by increasing your awareness of your own unique perspective. While we often think of creativity as being related to the arts, practically anything can be creative by looking at familiar things in a new way.

The first draft.

Most types of communicating begin with writing a first draft to get your ideas down on paper and getting started can be the most difficult part. Facing a blank page can be a daunting task, so start with what you know. Don't worry about getting it right the first time. Once you get something written down on paper, you can decide what works and what doesn't. Ask for feedback from people whose opinion you value.

Starting at the beginning is not necessarily the best approach. Start with what you know, start in the middle, or start with what's easiest for you to write to get things moving. Don't worry about getting things perfect, like writing the perfect opening line. If you get stuck don't get bogged down, skip over what's giving you a problem and write something else.

It's more important to keep moving because you can always come back to something and fix it later. Breakup big sections into smaller parts to make them more manageable and easier to write. Ideas don't necessarily come all at once, but have to be worked out over time.

Refining your message.

After the first draft is written, it needs to be refined. This is the process of rewriting, editing, and proofreading.

• Rewriting. Once you have your Great Idea on paper, take a step back to look at the big picture. Make sure that you have included everything you want to include. Make sure the information and evidence supports your central idea. Remove any unnecessary information that does not fit your topic or support your claim.

This is a good time to change the organization of ideas, sentence structure, or paragraph organization if needed. Paragraphs should follow in logical order using a method of organization. Transitions should be smooth so that one idea flows into the next. The introduction should properly introduce your subject to your audience and the conclusion should wrap everything up.

• Editing. Once everything is where it should be you can start checking the details. This involves rewriting sentences and paragraphs if necessary. Sentences and paragraphs should contain one clearly developed idea. Paragraphs should begin and end at natural breaks and follow logically based upon a method of organization.

Each paragraph should clearly relate to the preceding and following paragraph to create a flow of information that people can easily follow. Use a thesaurus to find the best words to express your ideas and a dictionary to check that words and terms are used correctly.

• Proofreading. This is the most detailed part of the editing process, which is why it is a specialized skill. Here you are not so much changing sections or words, but looking for errors. When you proofread you check for errors in spelling, punctuation, grammar, and proper word usage.

This is the fine tuning of the message to be sure it's written properly in the proper format. While it's helpful to have correct usage of grammar, some forms of communicating use informal rules to be better understood or sound more realistic.

Delivering Your Message

Once you have crafted your message you need to get it to your audience. In the process of communicating, you take your Great Idea and communicate it to others through a connection. The method of delivery is how you send a message through a connection. It can be spoken or written, verbal or nonverbal.

To communicate more effectively with others, it can be helpful to practice and rehearse your communicating skills. Whether you are giving a speech, producing a video, or presenting a musical performance, practice and rehearsal are essential to success.

Practice is repeating basic skills to develop a proficiency doing something. Rehearsal is running through an actual performance or presentation.

This helps to develop important skills by repeating them over and over to become proficient. Doing this can help give you confidence to improve your performance.

Rehearsal is preparing for a performance in front of an audience. A rehearsal should approximate the actual performance conditions as much as possible. For example, before a concert a musical group will rehearse to make sure that everything will go smoothly at the performance.

Rehearsing your message helps you to discover any unforeseen problems and reduces uncertainty about your performance. It helps to give you confidence to feel more comfortable during your performance because it will feel more familiar.

When speaking or giving a presentation you can utilize one of these delivery methods.

- Full text. Speakers often use a full written transcript of their speech. Newscasters and politicians read the full text from a teleprompter, so they say what is written and don't miss any words.
- Outline. This can be in the form of sentences, short phrases, or key words. This works when you know the material well enough, so you don't need a script to keep you on track.
- Memorization. This is giving a speech from memory without using any notes. It can sound more genuine, but can be risky if you forget your lines.
- Impromptu. This involves speaking spontaneously and unrehearsed without an outline or a script. This is the way we generally communicate with others.
- Extemporaneous. This is when we know what we are going to say, so we perform without any outline or notes. When we speak this way we sound more relaxed and genuine.
- Conversational. This style involves speaking informally as if you are engaged in a casual conversation with another person.

Vocal elements.

Vocal variety is changing how you speak to make it interesting to your audience. This includes changing your pacing, pitch, intonation, and volume to add variety to how you sound. Not using vocal variety can make you sound monotone and boring.

An important part of an effective delivery is pronunciation and articulation. Pronunciation is saying words the right way and articulation is saying them clearly. We add extra nonverbal sounds and intonation to what we say in order to communicate how to interpret our words. We alter our delivery to convey our attitude, mood, tone, and emotions.

Vocal elements.
* Pitch. This is how we use the high and low tones of our voice. We use pitch to emphasize emotions or make our voice more pleasing.
* Pacing. This is how fast or slow we speak. Changes in pacing can alter the emotional tenor of what we say. Fast pacing is more exciting and slow pacing can be more dramatic.
* Rhythm. Repeating certain sounds, words, or phrases can be used rhythmically for dramatic effect to sound like poetry or music.
* Pauses. These are periods of silence when we stop speaking between words or ideas. They are used for dramatic effect to emphasize ideas. They can also give us a chance to take a breath and compose ourselves before continuing.
* Volume. This is how loud or soft we speak. This can change based on the size of the room. It can be used to emphasize important ideas or to create different emotional effects. Changing volume helps to make what we say more interesting to your audience.
* Intonation. This is the vocal timbre or quality of our voice. It can vary from rich and full to thin and hoarse.

Nonverbal expressions.

Nonverbal expressions are important to visually maintain an audience's interest. They can be used to establish credibility because if you look confident, people are more likely to perceive you as credible. When you are aware of how nonverbal expressions work, they can be utilized to enhance your message.

• Facial expressions. We use them to communicate emotions like when we are happy, serious, or sad. Facial expressions can be used to emphasize important points. We make inferences about others based on their facial expressions including how they feel and the motivation for their behavior.

• Eye contact. We use eye contact to make connections with others. We use it to make inferences about them. When we are apprehensive we might avoid making eye contact. This can create the perception that we are indifferent, bored, or are not trustworthy. When someone looks you in the eye you feel that they are competent and confident about themselves and their message. Appropriate eye contact is a matter of degree, using too much can be as uncomfortable for others as too little. It's important to make appropriate eye contact with others because of what it can communicate to them.

• Gestures. We use gestures to communicate information in addition to what we say. While this can include how we use all parts of our body, it generally refers to how we use our arms and hands. Gestures are useful to emphasize important verbal points in a visual manner. They can serve the same function as underlining or using exclamation marks.

Many gestures have their own meaning like pointing, waving, or giving the thumbs up. Using gestures effectively is a matter of appropriateness and balance. Too many can make you look nervous, too few will make you look stiff and un-comfortable. Natural gestures can add the perception of confidence and forced gestures can make you look stiff or unnatural.

• Hands. It can be difficult to know what to do with your hands because they can feel awkward or get in the way. Rest them gently on the podium or table in front of you, if you can. If there's nothing to rest them on, hold them down at your sides with your elbows slightly bent.

Doing this can feel uncomfortable because we rarely stand this way, but it looks good in front of an audience or on camera. Sometimes people clasp their hands loosely together in front of them and gesture occasionally. Avoid putting them in your pockets.

• Stance. When you are out in public and have to stand in one place for awhile, like in front of an audience, you want to be comfortable and look confident. Stand up straight with your shoulders slightly back. Place your feet at a 45 degree angle with your heels a couple of inches apart, so your feet are spaced about the same distance as your shoulders.

Your knees and elbows should be slightly bent otherwise you may pass out if you stand too rigid. Stand straight, head up, shoulders back, and arms at your side.

• Posture. Posture is how you hold yourself and bearing is how you stand or move. These are important because people make judgments about you based on what they perceive. Having good posture communicates confidence and credibility.

Having good bearing means moving about with confidence and authority. Avoid shuffling your feet, rocking back and forth, or leaning up against something like a wall. When people do this we perceive them as lacking confidence or not being trustworthy.

• Movement. Whenever you are in front of an audience you will have to move. You may need to get on and off stage or move around while you are speaking. Movement includes how you do things like picking up your feet when you walk. It looks better to pick up your feet by bending the knee very slightly instead of shuffling them.

How much you move depends upon the space available, your message, and the occasion. Some movement is good because it makes you look animated. Too much movement will make you look nervous.

Use movement to emphasize important points. If you are telling an emotional story you might move closer to your audience because it's more personal. Afterwards, you will want to move back to a more public distance.

• Appearance. People make judgments about the credibility and competency of others based upon their appearance. The best approach is to dress appropriately for the occasion to enhance the audience's impression of you. When you are in front of other people you are a leader and should look the part. A good approach is to dress conservatively, slightly more formal than your audience.

• Act natural. It may take practice to act natural. Use nonverbal behavior to help you, but use it sparingly and intentionally. This can make the difference between looking confident or looking nervous, looking professional or looking like you don't know what you're doing.

While we shouldn't judge a person's message by how they look, the reality is people do. People make judgments based upon nonverbal behavior motivated by uncertainty. They are looking for information to better understand and evaluate what a person has to say and their appearance is often all they have to go on.

Anxiety.

When we communicate in public it's natural to feel a certain amount of anxiety. Anxiety has been called many things including nervousness, apprehension, and stage fright. These are all emotional expressions of uncertainty. We become anxious or apprehensive about something because the level of uncertainty is higher than we are used to making us uncomfortable.

Because of uncertainty, we are more likely to be anxious about not knowing what might happen than if we know what will happen, even if it's not good. This is because we can be better dealing with the adversity we know rather than with the uncertainty we do not know.

One of the best ways to reduce anxiety is by reducing uncertainty.
• We can do this by gaining experience through practicing communicating skills and rehearsing our presentation.

- We can use feedback to increase our awareness of how we are being perceived by others.
- We can utilize relaxation techniques like positive visualization or controlled breathing.
- If a mistake is not obvious, just keep going because chances are nobody will notice unless you tell them.
- If a mistake is obvious, you might stop and say you need a moment or acknowledge the mistake and briefly make light of it as if it's part of the presentation, then move on.
- It can help to expect that there will be some mistakes, so you can be prepared for them.

**A small amount of anxiety can be good because it can
give us energy, heightens the senses, and increases our awareness.**

A common source of anxiety comes from making eye contact with an audience. Making eye contact is an important part of making a connection with your audience, so it's helpful not to stare at your notes or the floor because your audience will be less receptive to your message.

If you are nervous about making eye contact, look at the tops of people's heads moving your gaze slowly around the audience. This gives the impression of making eye contact. Eye contact is important because it establishes a connection and your credibility with an audience, as well as providing you with feedback on how you are coming across to them.

We rarely tell people that we are feeling nervous, instead we communicate it through our nonverbal body language. We do this with the lack of eye contact, shifting back and forth, putting our hands in our pockets, jiggling keys or coins, touching our hair, rubbing our nose, crossing our arms, speaking rapidly, using a higher pitch, or speaking softly.

While you cannot control how you feel, you can develop skills to control what you do. By being aware of your nonverbal behavior and having options you can do things to avoid appearing as if you are nervous.

Your presentation.

When you speak in front of an audience your message begins when you start to speak, but your presentation begins the moment you arrive. When you arrive be warm, friendly, and polite because people may be forming their impressions of you. How you conduct yourself beforehand can make a difference in how receptive they are when you speak.

When you go up to speak, communicate confidence through good posture and bearing. Before you begin speaking take a moment to compose yourself, take a breath to relax, set up your outline, adjust your posture, and take control of the situation. Memorize the first few lines you are going to say so that you can say them with confidence to give you a solid start. If the beginning is solid, you will be perceived as confident. If the beginning is not solid, it may be difficult to recover.

This approach helps you to reduce uncertainty. It gives you a chance to familiarize yourself with your surroundings before beginning your presentation. It gives you a chance to relax and bolster your confidence. Avoid rushing or being in a hurry to begin because it can cause you to be off balance getting things off to a bad start.

Avoid saying things like "before I begin" or "my topic today." Avoid meaningless words including ahhh, like, or you know. We use these words because we are nervous or because we are not sure what to say. Practice and preparation should eliminate these problems.

Adapting to change.

You are in the middle of speaking to an audience, however, it's becoming clear that things are not going well. Now what do you do? This is when having awareness and options can help.

- Being aware of your audience can provide feedback to help you determine what to do.
- You can change or adapt your message or delivery to be more receptive to your audience.
- If your audience looks lost or confused you may be going too fast for them, so slow down your pacing.
- You might review information you already presented by rephrasing it in a different way or provide an illustration or example to increase understanding.
- You can make changes by telling different stories, using different illustrations, or adding new ideas based on feedback from your audience.
- If the audience is getting bored or restless move around, use a few more gestures, tell a personal story, wrap things up, or take a break if you can.

Increasing your awareness helps you to be ready for the unexpected.

We plan for things to go right, but we don't necessarily plan what to do if they go wrong. By anticipating what might go wrong, you can be prepared to make changes during your presentation. Be flexible by giving yourself options for change, so you are not forced to stick with one approach. Don't be reluctant to change what you have prepared if circumstances warrant.

Practice and rehearsal should include alternatives, so you can have them ready if needed. All too often we get locked into one way of doing things because it makes us feel comfortable. Practicing more than one way of delivering your message gives you alternatives.

Chapter 3
Be Smarter in Your Profession

Professional communicating is how we communicate for our job or career. It includes verbal skills like public speaking, motivational speaking, and making presentations. It includes written skills like writing a résumé, proposals, presentations, press releases, newsletters, or reports. These skills are important because regardless of the nature of the job, people need to communicate with one another.

Communicating skills are increasingly essential to career success.

Professional writing is generally more formal than other forms of communicating. It has established formats and uses proper form and structure including complete sentences and paragraphs with clear methods of organization. It uses proper grammar, accurate spelling, punctuation, and a professional vocabulary. It uses an appropriate tone that is more formal than speaking.

Professional writing should look professional by using the proper format and avoiding clutter to make it easy to read by having an appropriate amount of open space. Avoid using unusual type fonts, instead use a traditional font like Times Roman or Helvetica, so it looks professional and is easy to read.

Written Communicating

Correspondence, like writing a letter, includes the heading; sender's name and address; date; recipient's formal name and title; salutation or greeting; the body, which is your message; closing or ending; signature; and copies or enclosures.

Use the process outlined earlier to write the body of the letter. Keep it to one page in length because people may not read any further. Near the beginning of your letter clearly state in one sentence the reason you are writing. Near the end write the action you want taken.

A résumé is a form of identity management communicated to others in writing. It is an inventory of your education, experience, and skills that has the desired outcome of getting you a job. Know your recipients needs and wants so you can tailor your résumé to meet them. You can do this by knowing as much as you can about the recipient and by getting a copy of the job description, which is a written set of duties and responsibilities for the position.

Since many applications are sent over the internet, omit any information that you feel is too personal, that you don't want on the internet, or made public, like your home address. Use searchable key words and relevant technical jargon to help set your résumé apart.

These are some things to include in a résumé and cover letter.

1. Personal information. This includes your name, title, and how to contact you. You can use an email address or post office box.

2. Educational information. This includes degrees and educational institutions as well as training that applies to the position. Also include relevant honors or awards. Describe any skills or knowledge you have that is relevant to the job.

3. Employment information. This includes your past experience, job titles, dates, accomplishments, responsibilities, and employers. Let the reader know about your skills and accomplishments. Reduce uncertainty by letting them know what you did to encourage them to invest in you by telling them what you can do for them. Use active rather than passive language to share meaning by creating a picture of you in their mind.

4. Accomplishments. This includes awards, professional associations, and other honors relevant to the job. Leave out those that don't apply.

5. Career objectives. Some résumés include an optional career objective or general statement of purpose. Include this only if it's expected in your field or the job application asks for it. For instance, some professions like teaching might ask you to include your philosophy of teaching.

6. References. It has become accepted to put "references provided upon request," so have a separate sheet of references or letters of recommendation you can provide if requested.

7. Cover letter. Résumés are accompanied by a cover letter that should state the specific position you are applying for, why you are applying, and what you have to offer. End the letter by requesting a meeting or interview. Limit it to one page unless they specifically ask for more information.

The desired outcome of your cover letter is to get them interested in reading your résumé and to reduce uncertainty about you, so that they will contact you to set up an interview.

Interviews

There are many different types of interviews. These can include applying for a job, performance review, or being considered for a raise or promotion. You might be interviewed by the media, for a publication, on the radio, or on television.

While each has a different purpose, you can utilize similar communicating skills to achieve your desired outcome. Even though another person will be asking the questions, it is important for you to be in control of the situation.

**While you can't control what happens,
you can control what you say and do.**

The following can help you communicate more effectively.

• Reduce uncertainty. Perhaps the single most important thing you need to do is to reduce uncertainty in the mind of the person interviewing you, and the audience if there is one, because this can be the biggest obstacle to achieving your desired outcome. You can do this by using identity management. Consider what aspects of yourself and your experience are most appropriate to present to others in public.

• Share meaning. When we share meaning with others we make a connection that creates a common bond. One of the ways we do this is by talking about our past experiences. This reduces uncertainty because others can relate their experiences to ours. In an interview, it's important to fully consider what you want to talk about beforehand. It should be appropriate to the situation and not be overly personal.

In a job interview, you might talk about your experiences in other jobs. In a media interview, you want to share meaning with the audience, so they will understand your message. Talk about something familiar that they can relate to.

• Encourage investment. In order to achieve your desired outcome it's helpful to give the other person an incentive to invest in you to encourage them to hire you. In a media interview, you want the larger audience to invest in your message. You can encourage others to invest in you by reducing uncertainty through appropriate use of self-disclosure. Find a need they have and offer a way to fulfill it.

In a job interview you might talk about your responsibilities, problems you over-came, or your accomplishments. The person interviewing you may relate to your experiences and share their own stories creating shared meaning. In a media inter-view, you might share a personal story about you that is appropriate to the topic.

• Perceptions and expectations. Whether it is for a job, or a media interview like being on television, the interview process is a means by which we manage other people's perception of us. We communicate in specific ways in order for others to have a perception of us that supports our desired outcome.

Others use the perception process to develop their expectations of who we are and what we will do in the future. If they feel that we will fulfill their expectations, they can be more receptive to our desired outcomes, like hiring us for the job.

• Personal appearance. Find out what is expected for the situation and dress ap-propriately. This could mean work clothes, a suit, or uniform. You want to com-municate that you care about others because you made an effort to look good for them. Your appearance communicates information to others nonverbally, so be aware of what you communicate.

• Speaking. It's not just what you say, it's how you say it. Speak in a relaxed, con-versational, and purposeful manner. Speak with normal pacing, slightly lower the pitch of your voice, and use vocal variety to sound interesting. Avoid speaking too fast or too slow or raising the pitch of your voice.

When people ask you questions, be ready with answers. Waiting too long to an-swer can give the impression that you are not being totally forthcoming. Keep answers short, honest, and to the point. Do not say too little or too much.

• Nonverbal body language. Your nonverbal body language can communicate con-fidence and professionalism or nervousness and inexperience. Communicate con-fidence by moving in a purposeful manner using proper posture and good bearing.

Make appropriate eye contact and orientate your posture toward others to show that you are interested in them. Avoid communicating nervousness nonverbally by fidgeting, shuffling your feet, jingling keys, not making eye contact, or touching your clothes or face.

• Awareness. By having an awareness of how the process of communicating works, you can use reflected feedback to infer how others perceive you through their verbal and nonverbal behavior. Awareness of what they say and do can work as a kind of mirror that lets you know how you are doing. However, this is a matter of balance. Having too much self-awareness can make you seem self absorbed and having too little can make you seem out of touch or self centered.

• Anticipate their questions. Before any interview, write out a list of potential ques-tions that you might be asked so you can be prepared with your answers. Practice interview techniques and rehearse questions out loud to help you sound relaxed and confident, so you will be perceived as competent and professional.

• Answering questions. Whether it's a job interview or interview in the media, keep your answers to the point and avoid getting off topic. You may not know the questions they will ask ahead of time, but you can prepare some potential ques-tions and practice your answers beforehand.

If you are asked a question you don't know the answer to, don't lie or make it up. Most information can be easily verified. If there is something you don't know, don't say you don't know, say that you will have to get back to them with more information. Don't feel pressured to say something you shouldn't that you might regret later.

In an interview it is helpful to do the following.

Arrive early, so you have time to relax, check your appearance, and review what you are going to say. They may show you around so you can talk to others and ask questions that can provide helpful information.

Be polite, friendly, and courteous to everyone including the staff like receptionists and security personnel. Use self-disclosure to your advantage by sharing little bits of information that are relevant and appropriate to the situation. Opening up and sharing a little bit about a common interest may improve your chances of success and put everyone at ease.

Be flexible, but always stay in control of yourself even when things don't go as you expect. If the other person does not speak don't feel compelled to talk to fill the silence. This is a technique that can be used to get people to talk and say things they otherwise might not say. If this occurs you might ask them if they have any other questions.

Ask them questions. At the end of an interview you may be asked if you have any questions. Always have a few questions ready to ask. This is your opportunity to gain insight that can be useful whether you get the job or not. It's a way for you to give them positive feedback and get some feedback about yourself. They may do this to test you. If you do not ask any questions, it could seriously damage your chances of success because it communicates indifference and that you are not really interested in them, whether it's true or not.

Know your boundaries ahead of time including what you are willing to talk about or do and what you are not, then stay within them. If they ask you something you consider inappropriate ask why they consider it relevant or politely decline to answer. Be aware of what questions they can and cannot legally ask you. Stay within the prearranged time even if they do not. If they go past it, say that you don't want to keep them too much longer.

Thank them and express your appreciation for taking time to meet with you when you first meet and at the end of the interview. When you are finished ask them what happens next. This is an open ended question to encourage them to tell you about their plans and perhaps about other interviews.

If they seem receptive, get them to talk about the interview process and the criteria they use to make a decision. Ask them when you can expect to hear back from them. Then if you do not hear back it's an opportunity to contact them again.

If you are serious about creating a professional relationship, mail a hand written thank you note. Keep it simple, plain, classy, and to the point. If you don't hear anything, you might follow up by asking them where they are in the decision making process. They may be waiting to see if you are interested enough to follow up.

If you don't get the job you want, consider it a good experience to help you gain important information into the process and how others perceive you. This can give you another opportunity to contact them by sending a follow up letter or call expressing your disappointment and asking them about other opportunities.

Presentations

A useful communicating skill is the ability to prepare and present a report. There can be several tasks involved in doing this including writing the report, making a presentation, responding to questions, and using visual elements.

• The written report. A written report can be comprised of several parts. It can include a table of contents, background information, the methodology used to collect information, the criteria for analyzing the information, the process of preparing the report, and lastly the findings, conclusions, or recommendations. Some reports begin with an executive summary, which is a short description of the most important parts of the report. It may also include a cover letter that introduces the report. Utilize the process described earlier to create the report.

• The presentation. When a report is completed it may be accompanied by a presentation. The purpose is not to read the report, but to summarize important points. The report and any accompanying materials like the cover letter, executive summary, and any visuals or appendices should be distributed to everyone before the presentation so they have time to read them. A presentation can be made by one person or a group. It is written beforehand and rehearsed so it sounds professional. It can cover additional issues that may not be addressed in the report and often allows time for the audience to ask questions.

• Question and answer time. Part of the time allotted for a presentation may be set aside for the audience to ask questions. This serves two purposes. First, it gives the audience an opportunity to provide feedback about the presentation and the report.

Second, it gives the audience a chance to learn more about the report. The presenters should anticipate possible questions and practice their answers beforehand, so they can be prepared for them. Questions should be answered honestly, concisely, and professionally within the framework of the presentation. If you don't know an answer don't say so, say you will have to get back to them with more information.

An important skill is being able to write, coordinate, and make a group presentation. Group presentations are created and written using the process as outlined earlier. This can be challenging because instead of one person doing everything, the tasks of gathering information, organizing, writing, and presenting are divided between several people. Having several people give the presentation means that the work can be shared, more information can be gathered, and more ideas can be generated.

However, it can be difficult coordinating everyone, making decisions takes more time, and there may be conflicts. Things can run smoother with clearly defined responsibilities, a timetable, a process to make decisions and resolve disputes, and a desired outcome that everyone agrees on. The work should be divided so everyone feels they are making a fair contribution.

Rehearse the presentation as if you were really giving it before you actually give it. This is a good way to work out any problems so they don't happen later. Have a checklist to be sure nothing is missing or falls between the cracks.

Group work can be done collectively with everyone making decisions together or it can be divided up with tasks assigned to specific individuals who work on them on their own. Then, everyone comes back to the group to put their individual work together. Most groups work in some combination between the two like dividing the workload, but making decisions together.

Visual elements.

There are times when the written or spoken word does not provide the necessary information to communicate your message. So, you will need the help of visual elements because they provide another way to share meaning with your audience.

Visual elements are used in many forms of communicating like a speech, meeting, video, television show, on the internet, or in giving a presentation.

People are more likely to remember something when it is communicated through more than one connection. You can communicate information more effectively with a written report that is presented verbally and illustrated graphically.

Numbers printed on paper or statistics read aloud may be difficult to comprehend, but depicting them visually in a chart can make them easier to understand. This is because people perceive information in different ways. Some people are more receptive to listening, some to what they read or see visually, and others to what they experience.

When you communicate with others utilizing more than one connection they are more likely to understand you. Visual elements provide an additional connection to reinforce your message. Visuals help to share information that can be difficult to communicate in other ways.

For instance, we can describe how our circulatory system works, but it is not as effective as a photograph or diagram showing what it looks like. Visual elements make presentations more interesting for the audience. Professional looking visuals enhance your credibility and can make people more receptive to your message.

In order to communicate more effectively, it can be helpful to be familiar with the following options for visual elements.

• Electronic equipment. This includes audio visual equipment like a video projector, slide projector, film projector, overhead projector, audio tape, videotape, or a computer. These items need access to electricity, so they should be set up and tested ahead of time to be sure they work properly.

• Standalone. These visuals can be seen on their own so they need no electricity or additional technology. They include charts, graphs, maps, diagrams, schematics, and enlarged photographs. They are often put on an easel or hung on a wall. They should be easy to read and use where everyone can see them.

• Impromptu. These are visuals that are created during the presentation like writing on a marker board, chalkboard, or flip chart on an easel.

• Handouts. An alternative to large visuals is to provide handouts. The advantage is that everyone has a copy they can look at, write notes on, and take with them afterwards. This can include an outline, charts, graphs, visuals, or photographs. Handouts are often used with visuals like a powerpoint presentation.

• Tangible. These are tangible items that you can use to demonstrate or show to your audience. They can include physical three dimensional items like the actual item or a model representing it. If it is small enough you might pass it around the audience. If it's too big to pass around, place it where everyone can see it.

• Living beings. There are some times when it can be helpful to bring a living being as a visual element. For example, using a person to model clothing or a dog to demonstrate dog training.

**Visual elements should look professional
and be interesting to gain and keep the audience's attention.**

- They should be large enough to be seen by the entire audience.
- They should use bright colors, a simple typeface, and plenty of open space to make them easy to read.
- They should be concise, to the point, and support the topic.
- They should be easy to understand so you don't have to spend a lot of time explaining them.
- They should be designed for maximum impact on the audience, but not distract from the message or the speaker.

Arrive early to set up any visuals before the audience arrives. Place them so they are easy for you to reach and everyone can see them. Test them out ahead of time to make sure they work. Items like slide projectors and audio or video tapes should be queued so they are ready to go. Rehearse with your visuals beforehand and have a backup plan in case of unexpected problems like an equipment malfunction.

Speaking in Public

Speaking in public includes forms of communicating in audio visual media like video, television, and the internet as well as a personal appearance in front of an audience like a speech or presentation. For example, giving a speech involves both writing what you are going to say and then saying it in front of an audience.

When speaking in public, your desired outcome is to reduce uncertainty about yourself and your message, so your audience will be receptive to what you have to say. Then, you will want to share meaning with them so that they will understand your message. You may even want them to invest in your message by agreeing with you or taking some action afterward.

Consider your audience's desired outcome by acknowledging them and why they are there in your remarks. Be aware of their expectations and why they are listening to you, so you can fulfill them. Set the proper mood and tone for the occasion. Mention any connections between yourself and your audience, the significance of the event, and why everyone is gathered.

These are some common formats for speeches.

• Ceremonial speeches are given on special occasions like birthdays, weddings, anniversaries, and other important events. They can be used to commemorate a person, place, organizations, or important date. Be sure to mention the significance of the occasion, the people involved, the circumstances around it, and why everyone is there even though everyone may already know this.

• Inspirational speeches or sermons are usually spiritual in nature often based upon a religious text. Motivational speeches have the desired outcome of encouraging people to take action. They are often based upon real life experiences like overcoming adversity. Their purpose is to inspire or motivate the audience by utilizing the power of shared meaning to communicate shared values and beliefs.

• Tributes remember and share mutual experiences about a person or event. They are warm and sincere because they celebrate and acknowledge the contributions of others.

• Dedications usually commemorate a structure like a building, statue, or monument usually named to remember an important person. Be sure to recognize the significance of the event, the reasons for the dedication, and the audience. This can include historical references, anecdotes, or the reason for the dedication.

• Eulogies are usually given at a memorial service or funeral. They can include the positive attributes and accomplishments of the person being honored. They are generally serious and somber in tone, but can be lightened with personal stories.

• Toasts are a short tribute to a person given at a dinner. Everyone is asked to raise a glass to the person being toasted. They can include positive attributes about a person as well as humorous anecdotes.

• An after dinner speech is a humorous speech given after a dinner or banquet that can include entertaining stories about the experiences of the speaker and people in attendance.

These are several different types of speeches that can be given on separate occasions or they can take place during a single event like a convention or seminar.

• Convention speeches are usually given during an organized event attended by large numbers of people, like a business or political convention. They often involve a variety of speeches including a welcome address, introductions, keynote speech, awards, and nominating and acceptance speeches.

• Welcome remarks are often given at the beginning of an event to establish a positive tone by recognizing the nature of the occasion, why everyone is there, and to thank everyone for attending the event.

• Introductions are a short speech to introduce another person. Be brief, accurate, acknowledge the occasion, include important information about them relative to the occasion, and say their name pronouncing it correctly.

The purpose of an introduction is to inform your audience about the person you are introducing, to create a positive atmosphere, and get the audience ready to hear what they have to say. You can say good things about them that they cannot say themselves.

• Being introduced. When someone introduces you, be sure to thank them for their kind introduction and the audience for being there. This creates a positive atmosphere to help make them more receptive to your message.

• A keynote address is the most important speech at an event. It is often given by a noteworthy person to encourage people to attend. It is important to be positive and uplifting because it can set the tone for the event.

• Awards consist of two parts. First, the presenter tells about the award, why it is being given, and why the recipient is receiving it. Second, the recipient should thank those who may have helped them achieve the award. Be brief, to the point, and be humble.

• Nomination speeches recognize an individual for a position, to receive an honor or award, or to run for public office. They include describing the position, honor, award, elected office, or reason for the nomination.

• Acceptance speeches are given to accept a nomination, thank the people who helped them, tell why they are running for office, or what they will do if elected.

Meetings

You may have attended meetings that left you feeling good with a sense of accomplishment, while other meetings felt like a complete waste of time. What made the difference was probably how the meeting was conducted.

**Meetings serve an important function because they
do more than just make decisions or accomplish tasks, they help
people work together more effectively, provided they are properly run.**

- Meetings help people get to know one another by reducing uncertainty.
- They help people to share meaning when they talk about themselves and their experiences.
- They help people to invest in one another and the group, so they can share resources to get the task done.
- They help to negotiate the responsibilities of the participants.
- They help to determine how things will be accomplished.
- They help to encourage members to take action to implement decisions.
- They help groups to solve problems and make decisions.
- They help the group to develop its norms and roles.
- They help to develop the skills and abilities of the participants.
- They help to communicate and enforce the rules.

How a meeting is conducted can help to increase member satisfaction fostering their commitment to the group. Many tasks could be accomplished by phone, email, or memos, but these don't have the same benefits as meeting face to face.

There are many types of meetings based on the group's desired outcome.

- Meetings can be used to accomplish a task, make decisions, solve problems, make plans, or disseminate information.
- Social meetings can improve a group's social climate, provide entertainment, mark significant events, and celebrate rituals and traditions.
- Creative meetings come up with new and innovative ways of doing things.
- Committee meetings are often a group of appointed members who make decisions for a larger organization.
- An annual meeting conducts the business of an organization, like selecting a board of directors.
- A conference is a series of meetings with presentations and speeches.
- A seminar is a meeting to provide information, education, or training.

For an effective meeting utilize the following elements.

• Purpose. A meeting should have a clear purpose that is understood by everyone who attends. Before scheduling a meeting determine if it is actually needed or if things can be done in other ways like with a phone call or email.

Determine a clear desired outcome for the meeting because some meetings are held out of habit or just to show that something is being done.

Unnecessary meetings can be a source of frustration by wasting people's time that undermines their satisfaction and commitment to the group.

• Location. The right location helps to ensure a successful meeting. The purpose of the meeting determines where it should take place. It should be a place that optimizes achieving a group's desired outcomes. Having a professional looking space encourages a professional climate rather than being in a space that is cluttered.

The room should be free from distractions, like extraneous noise. It should be the right size to accommodate the group so everyone is comfortable including having enough chairs, tables, and space to work. It should be suited to your specific needs like having a podium, microphone, easel, or flip charts if needed. On the day of the meeting, be sure the room has everything the participants will need like pens and paper, water and glasses, or refreshments like coffee.

• Agenda. This is a written list of all the items that will be discussed at the meeting in chronological order along with the time allotted for each. An agenda is essential to a successful meeting because it reduces uncertainty to help keep things on track and establishes the same expectations for everyone.

Avoid putting too many items on the agenda or people may feel overwhelmed. Stick to the allotted time or people may feel that their time is being wasted. The agenda should be written and distributed before the meeting, so that everyone can be ready to get the work done.

**Without an agenda, a meeting can become
a discussion without a purpose, wasting people's time.**

Meeting time. Finding a time when everyone can meet may be one of the biggest challenges to setting up a meeting. A successful meeting starts and ends on time. Keeping it as short as necessary helps keep the energy levels high maintaining everyone's attention.

If the meeting runs long, schedule breaks so everyone can stretch and walk around. If a meeting runs too long or does not end on time, it can make people feel frustrated. Instead, consider adjourning and take up the remaining items at another time.

For an effective meeting, participants should do the following.

• Come to the meeting prepared. Read the agenda and any attachments beforehand. Be prepared and informed about what is going to be discussed. If you have any questions call beforehand to clarify them so you don't waste time at the meeting.

• Arrive at least ten minutes early, so you can help with any last minute preparations. This gives you a chance to talk informally with others or take a few minutes to relax and compose your thoughts.

Few things undermine how people perceive you as much as arriving late because it communicates that you don't value their time, even though you do.

• Talk during the meeting, but have something substantive to say. Avoid dominating the conversation, but don't sit back either. Come prepared to contribute your ideas and ask questions. Organize your thoughts so you are clear and succinct. Write down anything you want to bring up so you don't ramble using up valuable time.

• Support and encourage others. If you think someone has a good idea, tell them. Utilize positive nonverbal behaviors like smiling and eye contact to show others that you are interested in what's going on.

• Listen to what others have to say. Because you have come prepared, you can listen to what they are saying rather than only thinking about what you are going to say next. Take notes so that you can respond to them at the appropriate time. Listening helps us make good decisions because we are better informed.

Conducting a meeting requires many of the qualities of being an effective leader. The following items provide a plan that can be adjusted or modified depending upon the type of meeting and your desired outcomes. Being a leader requires many of the same responsibilities as a participant, but there are a few other things to do.

To have an effective meeting, do these tasks in the following order.

1. Arrive before everyone else. Be sure the room is set up so everything is in place before the others arrive. Have the tables and chairs set up, pens and pads in place, water and refreshments available. Be sure everyone can see everyone else. Check the room temperature so that it is not too hot or cold, and the lighting is adequate.

Arrange any visuals so everyone can see them. Test any electronic equipment to be sure it is working properly. If there is a speaker, be sure there is a podium and microphone properly placed in working order.

2. Set up your place to sit. The person who conducts the meeting typically sits at the head of a boardroom table, the center of a long table, or at twelve o'clock for a round table. Place your agenda in front of you. During the meeting, check off each item as it is accomplished. Bring a clock that is unobtrusive and easy to read.

If you have a wristwatch, take it off and set it on the table next to your agenda. You can look at both at the same time to keep the meeting on track and no one should notice you checking the time. Looking at your watch when it's on your wrist could be interpreted to mean that you're bored or have someplace better to be.

3. Have someone welcome everyone as they arrive. You can do this, but you will probably be busy with last minute details. It's discouraging to show up for a meeting and no one talks to you. Welcoming everyone lets them know you're glad to see them and that they are valued. This sets a positive tone for the meeting and develops the social aspect of the group.

4. Allow social time. Schedule a few minutes of social time at the beginning and end of the meeting so participants can talk informally with one another. This utilizes the power of shared meaning and self-disclosure to reduce uncertainty by helping everyone to get to know one another so they can work better together. This can be a time to introduce newcomers to the other members.

5. Start the meeting on time. It's frustrating to show up on time and then wait for a meeting that starts late. Announce to everyone the meeting is starting and they should take their seats. Once everyone is seated, call the meeting to order. If you arrive late or the meeting starts late, be sure to apologize to everyone and provide a short, sincere reason why.

6. Begin with a welcome to let everyone know you appreciate them being there. Take a few minutes for everyone to introduce themselves. Write down their names in the order they are seated or pass around a sign in sheet so you can use their names when you call on them at the meeting. State the purpose of the meeting, expectations, and desired outcomes.

7. Briefly review the agenda to focus everyone's attention on the tasks ahead. An agenda helps you to keep the meeting on task and on time. Check off each item as it is covered. Make notes to keep track of what has been accomplished. Depending upon the type of meeting, you may need to follow parliamentary procedure including calling the meeting to order, roll call, reading of the minutes, committee reports, old and new business, making motions, and voting.

8. A record should be kept of what transpired at the meeting. This is usually done by someone other than the meeting leader. Groups often have a secretary who writes the minutes of the meeting that includes the date, beginning and ending times, items that were discussed, motions and decisions that were made, and actions taken.

9. The leader makes sure that everyone contributes and no one dominates the discussion. Encourage everyone to talk by going around the room and asking each person to contribute an idea. If decisions need to be made, utilize the decision making processes outlined in this book.

10. Keep the group on task to achieve the desired outcomes for the meeting. Wrap up discussions when they have gone on long enough by providing a summary of what has been decided so far. This will help members who may not have been paying attention know where they are and gives everyone a feeling of accomplishment because they are making progress.

You can get the group moving to the next item by saying something like, "The next item on the agenda is." If they are reluctant to move on remind them of the time limitations. Doing this should motivate them because nobody wants a meeting to run long.

11. When the meeting has concluded, summarize what has been done so everyone feels a sense of accomplishment. Review what actions are to be taken so everyone knows what they are supposed to do after the meeting. If possible, determine the date for the next meeting. Be sure to thank everyone for their time and good work. Then officially adjourn the meeting.

12. Allow some time after the meeting for members to socialize. If they feel they are pushed out of the room immediately after the meeting, they may not feel as good about it. Some may want to stick around and talk about the meeting while others may leave right away. This can be a good time to get some feedback from them about the meeting. People may be more willing to say what is on their mind because it is not in front of everyone else and the meeting is still fresh in their mind.

13. After the meeting, have the minutes typed up and a copy sent to everyone who was there and any members who were absent. Include the date of the next meeting or possible dates for it. Send a handwritten thank you note to any guests or speakers.

14. Once you have had a chance to relax and get some perspective, analyze the events of the meeting. Determine how well it went, review any feedback, and review the meeting minutes. This helps you to critically evaluate how well the meeting went. Ask yourself, what went well and what could be improved.

Communicating Skills

The following are skills that can be helpful to effectively communicate with others in a variety of situations.

1. Awareness is how we gather information through the perception process and how we use that information. We might feel that we are aware of what's around us because we notice things every day, however, awareness is a skill that can be developed. It involves developing our perception skills so that we notice more of what is around us.

Awareness includes self-awareness, which is knowing what we are communicating both verbally and nonverbally to others and how they perceive us. Increasing self-awareness can be difficult because we don't know what we don't know. In order to effectively communicate with others, it can be helpful to see yourself as others see you.

People in many professions increase their self-awareness. For example, public speakers or musicians might record themselves and then listen to their performances. Professional athletes may analyze videos of their games. Everyone has a different level of self-awareness. Balance is important because a high level of self-awareness can be self indulgent and a low level can make us seem indifferent.

Everyone can improve their awareness skills utilizing everyday activities.

Try this exercise. If you are sitting in a restaurant, coffee shop, at work, or just about anywhere, take a minute and close your eyes. Try to remember everything you can about your surroundings. What people are in the room? What do they look like? What is the room like? What kind of furniture is in it and where is it located? Then open your eyes and see how accurate you were.

Try keeping a small notebook with you to write down your observations and perceptions. For instance, after a meeting, a lunch, or going someplace like shopping, take a moment to write down everything you can remember. Write it down in as much detail as you can. Once you are done, if you can, look around and check your accuracy.

The purpose is to train your mind to be naturally aware of your surroundings. This can help you to communicate more effectively, have a greater understanding of yourself and others, and in extreme situations might save your life.

For example, could you describe someone to the police if you had to identify them? Could you find your way out of the room or building if you could not see, if the electricity went out, or there was smoke from a fire? Developing these skills can improve our competence and give us confidence in our abilities.

2. Options. Increasing our awareness can provide us with more options. Since there is no one right way to communicate in any given situation, having options helps us to communicate more effectively. Having options is not just about having choices, but having the ability to choose the best one in a given situation.

Having options can help us to not fall into the habit of doing the same things over and over when they may not be effective. It helps us to evaluate our ways of doing things to see what can be improved to be more effective. The more options you have, the better your chances are of achieving your desired outcome.

However, options are good up to a point, because having too many can be as problematic as too few. When we have too many options, we can become paralyzed with an inability to choose one. Most of the time we need only a few good choices. Awareness helps us to look at what works and why it works. Having awareness and options makes it possible for you to change or add new ideas and skills, so you can choose what works best for you.

3. Confidence. In effectively communicating with others it is helpful to have confidence and competence. Confidence is about our believing in ourselves, our skills, and our abilities. It is the ability to develop our own self image and control how we present it to others. It is the ability to choose how we communicate with others so that they will understand us and respond positively. It is the ability to communicate effectively to achieve your desired outcomes.

People who speak clearly and with authority, who are knowledgeable, and are aware of themselves and others as well as the situation are often perceived as being confident. People are more likely to be receptive to someone who shows confidence because it makes them feel safe and secure by reducing uncertainty.

4. Competence. Competence is having a variety of skills and the ability to use them effectively. It is having an awareness of our own skills and knowledge of the options that are available to us. These skills can be based upon our experiences, education, and expertise.

Practicing these skills not only makes us better at them, it makes us more confident so we will be perceived by others as being more competent. People who are competent are seen as being more likable, organized, and professional. Having competence gives us the confidence to use our knowledge and skills to the best of our ability.

Competence provides the knowledge and skills to communicate effectively. Experience sharpens and refines those skills in actual situations. Confidence gives us a belief in ourselves and our abilities.

5. Range and repertoire. Range is the variety of notes produced by a musician, the area in which something can operate, or the distance something can travel. In communicating, range is the variety of skills you have to communicate effectively with people in many different types of situations.

In music, repertoire is the body of artistic works a musician is able to perform. In communicating, it can be the variety of resources, techniques, or skills available to communicate effectively with others. This gives you options and having options gives you the flexibility and freedom to make choices rather than reacting to the actions of others. Having range and repertoire provides a variety of options to make the right one for your particular situation.

6. Adaptability and Performance. Adaptability is having the expertise and capability to apply a variety of options and select the one that works best in a given situation. It's having the flexibility to move from one option to another if one doesn't work until a successful one is found.

Performance is having the expertise and capability to use communicating skills in real situations to communicate more effectively. Performance skills are developed through practice and experience.

People who are effective communicators have the ability to adapt and hone their approach to communicate differently based on the situation and individuals involved. To do this, it's helpful to break out of familiar patterns, to try new approaches, and to be aware of the feedback we receive from others.

Chapter 4
Be Happier by Reducing Uncertainty

We are born with needs we cannot fulfill ourselves, so they must be fulfilled by others for us to survive. These needs are fulfilled by our parents and family. So, we try to communicate our needs to others who try to understand them. Having needs that must be fulfilled motivates a lifelong process of communicating with others.

Some needs must be fulfilled to survive like food, clothing, and shelter. But we also have other needs and wants. We need safety, security, and stability. We have material needs like money and possessions. We want to have relationships with other people. We have spiritual, religious, and emotional needs. We need to know about ourselves, others, and the world around us.

We need to work and feel a sense of accomplishment, but we also need rest, enjoyment, entertainment, and fun. We may need prestige, status, and respect. We need to be ourselves or find self fulfillment. When people have some needs or wants fulfilled, they often need more. People can have virtually unlimited needs and wants, which are constrained by limited resources.

The nature of needs and wants.

We may feel frustration, depression, or tension in our lives and wonder why we feel this way. Tension is a natural part of life because it arises out of fulfilling our needs and wants. Unfulfilled needs and wants are uncomfortable creating tension.

We often have more needs and wants than we have resources forcing us to set priorities that can be difficult because it can leave some of them unfulfilled.

Some needs and wants cannot be fulfilled at the same time creating tension between them. By having an awareness of our needs and wants, and how they motivate behavior, we can reduce our feelings of frustration and tension.

By understanding how competing or conflicting needs and wants affect us we can find a balance to avoid unnecessary frustration or tension.

We have many conflicting needs and wants.
- We need to feel close to others, but we also need our own space.
- We need to belong to groups like our family, but we also need our own individual identity.
- We need safety and stability, but we also need adventure and excitement.
- We need to share information about ourselves to develop relationships, but we also need privacy.
- We need to work and be productive, but we want time off and have fun.

When we have conflicting needs and wants, we might feel tension or guilt. For example, if our family wants us to spend time with them, but we need some time to ourselves, we may feel guilt or tension.

How we perceive our needs and wants can be characterized in the following ways.
1. Compelling needs and wants. These motivate us to take action.
2. Competing needs and wants. These create tension between which one to choose.
3. Conflicting needs and wants. These can hinder us from taking action.

In order to better understand what motivates your behavior, make a list of your needs in order of importance. Do the same for your wants. Next to each one, on a scale of 1 to 10 write down how well you feel they have been fulfilled. Doing this can help increase your awareness of your needs and wants and how they motivate you. Not fulfilling some needs and wants can lead to unhappiness and tension leaving us feeling frustrated and depressed, but we may not know why.

Making a list can help you to determine what is important to you, so that you can more effectively allocate your time to fulfill more of them. It can help you spend less time doing things that make you end up feeling frustrated and spend more time doing things that make you feel fulfilled.

The Nelsonian Laws of Communicating.

It is difficult to talk about communicating without including behavior. Rarely do we communicate with someone and that's all. We communicate while we do things. We don't often do things without communicating about them and we don't often communicate without taking some kind of action.

Communicating and behavior are virtually inseparable because our behavior communicates information to others. How we communicate influences our behavior and the behavior of others. Our behavior has the ability to communicate information about us to others and the behavior of other people communicates information about them to us. So, when this book refers to communicating what is actually being described is behavioral communicating.

Behavior is better understood when we know why people communicate because it gives what they do meaning. This process of behavioral communicating consists not only of how people use behavior to communicate, but how communicating affects behavior.

How we communicate with other people is shaped by the forces that motivate human behavior. These laws influence our behavior to comprise a Grand Unified System of Human Behavior. Like the laws of physics, these laws have governed human behavior and how we communicate since the beginning of time. By understanding these laws and the forces they create, we can better understand human behavior and how we communicate.

The laws of behavioral communicating are analogous to the laws of nature and physics. They apply to everyone and do not change. These laws shape human behavior and how we communicate. They can be used to help understand what motivates human behavior including how and why we communicate with one another.

The author of this book is the first person to develop and apply new and innovative methodologies to understand how people are motivated by laws that govern communicating and behavior. The author of this book is the first person to identify these laws, the *Nelsonian Laws of Uncertainty, Shared meaning, and Investing*, which comprise a *Grand Unified Theory of Behavioral Communication*. These laws are in order of importance because the process begins with the first law and each preceding law is created by the ones before it.

Uncertainty

Life is uncertain. The world around us is chaotic. Things can happen with no warning or for no apparent reason. We may know that things might happen, but do not know when or how. No one can predict the future or has the ability to control everything that might happen. Despite our best planning things do not go as we expect. We experience things we do not want like illness, financial troubles, and natural disasters. We are aware of our own mortality, even though we do not know when or how it will happen. All these things create uncertainty.

The law of uncertainty is the first and most important law because it makes the other two laws possible. No matter how much people seek to reduce uncertainty, it cannot be totally eliminated. This is in part because we have needs and wants that must be fulfilled, because there are things about life we don't know, and because there are things that are out of our control.

Even if uncertainty could be totally eliminated, it would be detrimental for us and society. The law of uncertainty provides critical functions that shape who we are as individuals. Without uncertainty we would not be motivated to do the things that need to be done for society to function.

The degree of uncertainty we experience is based on our individual perspectives and experiences. What constitutes uncertainty for one person may be viewed as a challenge or adventure for another. Uncertainty is different for each person because it is based upon our past experiences, the degree to which our needs and wants are fulfilled, and the difference between our perceptions and expectations.

**Uncertainty is the difference between how much
security and stability we have in our life and how much we need to have.**

Uncertainty affects our self-concept and how we communicate with others based on the confidence we have in ourselves. This can include the difference between what we know and what we need or want to know. It can be the degree to which we feel we have some predictability about the future and having our expectations met. Uncertainty occurs when reality, or our perception of reality, does not meet our expectations. Uncertainty can be measured by the degree to which there is a gap between our expectations and our perception of reality.

Uncertainty reduction.

Uncertainty can be uncomfortable, painful, even intolerable. It can create feelings of tension, frustration, and even anger. When we are faced with something we do not like, that is uncomfortable, or painful we are motivated to reduce or eliminate it. This is how the law of uncertainty motivates people to reduce uncertainty through the process of uncertainty reduction.

We reduce uncertainty to reduce tension, frustration, and discomfort. Uncertainty reduction can help us to create predictability, stability, and security improving our quality of life. When bad things happen, we seek to understand them in order to reduce uncertainty and its impact on us.

Uncertainty motivates our behavior by forcing us to communicate with one another. It motivates us to take action to do things. If we had all the answers, we wouldn't have to look for them. Instead, we are forced to find them for ourselves leading to the creation of society as we know it today. Virtually everything that people do is motivated by their need to reduce uncertainty to fulfill their needs and wants.

By being unable to fulfill all our needs and wants, we are not always certain how they will be fulfilled. This creates uncertainty that can make us uncomfortable motivating us to take action. We want to know how our needs and wants will be fulfilled because we like stability and predictability, so we will be more comfortable.

In order to reduce uncertainty we have learned to communicate with one another, we have learned how to find out more about the world around us, and we have learned how to better understand ourselves. From the moment we are born, as well as from the beginning of human history, people have been motivated by uncertainty to learn about themselves and the world around them, so that they could fulfill their needs and wants.

A stop sign won't stop your car.

To illustrate how uncertainty affects our behavior, think about what you do when you are driving and see a stop sign or stop light. You have to see the sign, understand what it means, and then act accordingly. The sign does not stop your car, so why do you really stop? We stop because of the law of uncertainty. Because there's a chance you might get hit by another vehicle or be pulled over and given a ticket that would cost you money. We stop because it reduces uncertainty giving you reasonable expectations of getting safely across the road.

Uncertainty can be helpful.

While we spend much time and energy to reduce uncertainty, having a manageable level of uncertainty is preferable to completely eliminating it because having some uncertainty serves important functions for us as individuals and for society.

Uncertainty is important because it can open our mind to new ideas.
- It motivates us to question our assumptions to ascertain their validity.
- It motivates us to adapt and rethink what we already know.
- It motivates us to look at what we know in new ways to find something better.
- It motivates us to change and try something new.
- It motivates us to take action.

While uncertainty may not always happen in positive ways, it motivates us to look beyond what we already know. If everything worked out for us the way we wanted it to, we would be less likely to challenge ourselves, gain new knowledge, or open our mind to new possibilities.

However, we do not have to wait for difficulties caused by uncertainty to motivate us to look for new ideas and try new things. We can choose to open our mind and think about alternatives before we have to.

We can be open to new information and ideas to initiate change on our own terms rather than being forced to by circumstances. When we fail to take the initiative to do these things ourselves, life can have a way of making us do it.

Excessive uncertainty reduction.

When we are overly certain we know what to do, so we do not stop and consider alternatives that might provide better choices. Being overly certain can create may unnecessary problems.

When we are overly certain;
- We are not open to new information.
- We do not consider other ideas or alternative ways of doing things.
- We do not listen to others who may have something to contribute.
- We discount or filter out information that may be helpful.
- We are less likely to question our assumptions and the validity of information.
- We do not look for flaws in our reasoning or test the validity of our solutions.
- We do things the way that we want, instead of considering the ideas of others.
- We know that we are right and do not stop to think that we might be wrong.
- We do not need to learn anything new because we know what we are doing.
- We can become arrogant creating an attitude that "I know what I'm doing."
- We create conditions that can lead to bad decisions with disastrous results.
- We perceive people who have different ideas as disruptive troublemakers.

Shared Meaning

The law of shared meaning is the second law of behavioral communicating. It is like the law of uncertainty in that it is created by nature, so it affects everyone whether we want it to or not.

It affects how we communicate and share information with one another. It gives information significance to help make it useful to us. It helps us to understand and make sense of our experiences. It helps us to understand ourselves and develop our self-concept. It is how we find common ground to better understand others.

When something contains meaning it helps us access additional information from our experiences that may be useful, so we don't have to get all the information we need every time we communicate about something.

We are motivated by the law of uncertainty to create and share meaning, so that we can understand others to work with them and form relationships. This helps us to make sense out of our experiences to help explain what has happened in the past and better understand what we can reasonably expect in the future.

We invest symbols with meaning including words that makes language work. We give meaning to practically everything around us including other people, places, things, events, and ideas. Sharing meaning provides security and stability because we have a better understanding of the world around us.

Shared meaning is how we make sense of the world around us.

Our life consists of a series of experiences, but some may not make sense motivating us to wonder why they happen and what we should do about them. In order to reduce the uncertainty that would be created if these were perceived of as just random events, we want to understand them better by looking for meaning in them.

In order to do this, we may share our experiences with others to get their opinion about what happened to us and they may share their experiences with us in return. Sharing our experiences with others creates a mutual understanding, which gives us a deeper meaning reducing uncertainty that can help make similar situations more meaningful in the future.

Shared meaning provides a way to communicate with others to share information about ourselves. Much of how our identity is created is through our experiences and sharing meaning about them. How we communicate our experiences helps develop our own sense of self-concept and identity.

When we share our experiences with others they learn about who we are and we learn about them, which can help to reduce uncertainty, so that we can develop relationships with them.

How the law of shared meaning works.

You have likely experienced something that illustrates how the law of shared meaning works. Have you ever attended a party, wedding, or other event with a friend who knew everyone there, but you didn't know anyone?

They probably talked, laughed, and shared stories about mutual friends. If you didn't know anyone there you probably felt awkward, out of place, and maybe even wanted to leave.

What you observed is how the law of shared meaning works. The others were able to take what they communicated and add additional information increasing its meaning and significance making it more useful to them, while you probably didn't know what they were talking about. What you experienced is what things could be like if there was no shared meaning.

The law of shared meaning can be
illustrated by how we interpret information.

To demonstrate how this works, find a book that has pictures of people you know and another book that has pictures of people you don't know, along with their names and some kind of other information about them like a school yearbook.

Look at pictures of people you don't know. You can see what they look like, read their names, and understand the information about them. You probably won't have much additional information about who they are other than what is printed. Now look at the book with pictures of people you know.

Read their names and the information about them. You might recall things about them, things they did, perhaps even feelings or emotions. What you are thinking and feeling contains information that is beyond what is printed in the book.

When we see people we know, we recall things about them like the things that they did, perhaps even feelings or emotions. You might have feelings of warmth and affection or perhaps dislike or agitation. You might remember things that you did together that makes you laugh.

What you are thinking and feeling contains information that is beyond what is happening in the present. It's like a connection is made and something opens up. It's a very different experience than when we see or talk to people we don't know.

If there were no law of shared meaning, what we communicate to others would be more like looking at pictures of people we don't know. We could communicate with one another, but there would be little additional information available making it more difficult to understand them. We would have to explain practically every-thing every time we communicated.

Having shared meaning gives us a reserve of information that we can call up without having it explained every time we needed it. Shared meaning is how we make sense of the world around us.

It is how we interpret our observations, thoughts, feelings, and experiences. It shapes our view of practically everything because it influences how we see ourselves, others, and the world around us.

Investing

The law of investing is the third law of behavioral communicating. It is similar to the laws of uncertainty and shared meaning because it cannot be changed and affects everyone. It was formed by the other two laws in order to make them work.

We can reduce uncertainty and share meaning, but we need to take action for anything to happen. In order to reduce uncertainty and share meanings, we must invest our time and other resources in ourselves and others.

People may react to the first two laws by simply hunkering down and building a cabin in the woods to live. However, the law of investing forces them out into the marketplace of communicating. The law of investing regulates how we manage our resources and negotiate with others to fulfill needs and wants, so we can accomplish our desired outcomes.

This creates a kind of marketplace where people make and receive offers utilizing their resources to obtain their desired outcomes. Communicating is the currency of this marketplace because it enables us to invest these resources.

Investing makes human behavior work by connecting us to others.

We all have needs and wants that we cannot fulfill ourselves, so we need help from others to fulfill them. Other people also have their own needs and wants that they cannot fulfill themselves, so they also need help. This means people want things, but need help from others to obtain them.

Having our needs and wants fulfilled often comes at a cost. We have resources of value that others need and they have things we want. The most familiar resource is money, but we more often utilize other resources like our time, attention, effort, energy, expertise, experience, and skills.

When we have unfulfilled needs and wants it can be uncomfortable motivating us to communicate with others to achieve our desired outcomes.

When this process goes smoothly everyone can benefit, however, it often does not. People can have virtually unlimited needs and wants to fulfill with limited resources.

We often have conflicting needs and wants. We may feel we are contributing to others, but not receiving what we need in return. This can create tension, frustration, and even conflict, which can force us to make choices about our relationships and how we communicate with others.

For example, if we do not feel we are being fairly paid for the work we are doing, we might look for another job. If we feel we have been contributing to a relationship where the other person is only taking and our needs are not being met, we might want to breakup.

This is how the law of investing can motivate our behavior.

In order to invest in others we need to reduce uncertainty. When we feel a great deal of uncertainty, we are reluctant to invest our resources because we do not know what to expect in return. When we reduce uncertainty, we are more likely to invest so we feel safe and secure because we have reasonable expectations about what we will receive in the future.

The less uncertainty we feel the more comfortable we are sharing our resources in order to help others to fulfill their needs and wants. This also makes it more likely for them to help us fulfill ours. Not only do we seek to reduce uncertainty to invest, but we also invest to reduce uncertainty. We invest our resources in relationships and activities that will benefit us now and in the future.

For example, we invest time and energy in a job to receive not only a salary, but also for the safety and security that comes with it. This can help us to fulfill other needs like buying a house, having a family, or retirement.

The law of shared meaning helps us to invest because it increases our mutual understanding of one another. When we share meaning with others, we feel we get to know them better so we know what to expect of them in the future. This can increase stability and security making us feel more comfortable investing our resources.

The more we feel safe and secure, the more we are likely to invest ourselves and our resources in relationships without expecting an immediate return. This helps us to establish the long term stability necessary for creating and maintaining meaningful relationships.

Uncertainty affects us all. Instead of letting it control us, we can increase our awareness and have options to do something about it. Understanding how the laws of communicating work can help you to communicate more effectively with other people to create and maintain relationships, work in groups and organizations, and fulfill your needs and wants.

Chapter 5
Be Aware of The Rules of Communicating

The laws of uncertainty, shared meaning, and investing were created by nature to motivate human behavior. In order to utilize these laws, people developed rules for behavior and communicating.

Nearly all activities, groups, and organizations have their own set of rules to govern people's behavior. Rules help reduce uncertainty, so people know what is expected of them and what they can expect from others. Without rules we wouldn't know what to do and things would breakdown into chaos.

All groups have one thing in common, at one time they did not exist. Groups were created by people who got together to fulfill their needs and wants, and achieve desired outcomes. In order for them to do this they had to create rules to govern their behavior. As their needs and wants changed, the rules also needed to change.

These are several types of rules.

• Formal rules. Our behavior is governed by a set of formal rules that are written down in laws. These rules maintain order in society to reduce uncertainty. They tell people what they are supposed to do and have penalties for violating them.

• Constitutive rules. These are the rules that constitute proper behavior. They are the rules of how to play the game. They can be written down like in sports, but often they're not. These rules govern our behavior in most aspects of our lives.

• Regulatory rules. These rules are used to regulate people's behavior. They are a means to enforce the rules by providing penalties when they are violated.

• Practical rules. These are the rules of everyday behavior that everyone is expected to know. Sometimes they are formal like manners or etiquette. Other times they are advice about how to do something, like how to play tennis or golf. These rules are developed over time based on practical experience and are changed as needed.

• Rationale rules. These rules explain why rules exist and why they are important so people will follow them. In sports, rules provide for everyone's safety. Letting people know why the rules exist helps them understand why they need to follow them for their own benefit to encourage their compliance.

• Historical rules. Many groups and organizations have a history or traditions that are part of their heritage or identity. They can be used to attract people to join them. Historical rules were developed in the past and are often used to keep customs and traditions alive.

The nature of reality.

The laws of uncertainty, shared meaning, and investing were created by nature and the rules of communicating were created by people. Everything created by people at one time did not exist. These things first existed as an idea in a person's mind who had to communicate them to others who had to understand them in order to become reality.

This process of developing ideas and communicating them to others works not only for tangible things people create, but also for concepts and ideas. Often these ideas shape how people think and motivates their behavior creating physical reality. When people use this process to communicate their ideas to others, it helps to create social reality.

When we think of reality, we think of things like physical objects we can touch, which actually exist as opposed to something that exists in our mind. However, the thoughts and ideas that exist in our mind can become as much a reality as the tangible things around us. What we think about and communicate to others can create a reality of its own.

Social Reality

Social reality is how we make sense of the world around us.

Social reality determines how we explain, understand, and react to physical reality. It is created by people through the process of communicating with one another. People are motivated to create social reality by the law of uncertainty in order to reduce uncertainty. Social reality reduces uncertainty because it provides the information, structure, and rules people need to function in society.

Social reality shares meaning because it is an organized collection of people's experiences and behaviors. It allows investing because it creates stability so people know what to expect. It can be seen as an organized collection of rules, perceptions, and expectations we have of ourselves and each other.

Social reality can create physical reality. While social reality primarily exists in our minds, it can become as real as physical reality because of its power to motivate people's behavior. It is how we interpret the information we gather creating our perspective of how we see ourselves, others, and the world around us. It can be seen in the physical things people create.

Social reality changes over time changing our physical reality. Even though people's needs have remained much the same throughout history, how they fulfilled them has changed considerably. We need to wear clothes, but the way we dress is determined by what social reality tells us is acceptable. It once motivated women to wear corsets and men to wear tights.

Social reality can determine what ideas are considered acceptable and how we use them. Throughout history, people have formed governments motivated by similar needs for security and stability, but have created very different physical realities.

In ancient times, rulers claimed they were descended from the gods or ruled by divine right. Later, monarchs were chosen by birthright. More recently, leaders are elected by the people. Different social realities based on different cultures and time periods manifested themselves in different physical realities.

For example, everyone needs to eat, so we raise food crops that need rain to grow. In the past, people have interpreted the lack of rain that made for a poor harvest as God's displeasure with them. Some cultures responded with human sacrifices, others sacrificed animals, and others felt they needed to atone for their sins by praying more.

Today, we explain the lack of rain as being due to weather patterns, so we develop drought resistant crops and build irrigation systems. In each of these societies, different social realities explained the same physical reality in different ways motivating people to take different actions. This makes social reality very powerful, even potentially dangerous because it determines what people do about what they perceive.

The power of social reality is in its ability to
motivate behavior by affecting how we perceive physical reality.

Social reality helps to bring our thoughts and ideas into existence in physical reality. It affects people's behavior, actions, and how they communicate with others. Everything created by people first existed in someone's mind who, through the process of communicating, shared it with others. As more people shared the idea it became a part of social reality. Through their actions, it can create its own reality that can be as real as physical reality.

The Perception Process

Perception is how we gather information and give it meaning, so that it can be useful to us. We gather information through our five senses: sight, sound, taste, touch, and smell. We also gather information through other means like our feelings, emotions, intuition, and impressions.

Perception is the means by which we get to know what we know. It is how we make sense of the world and influences how we communicate with others. Everything we know and think including how we view ourselves and others is created through perception.

Perception is not only how we gather information, but how we come to understand it. It is how we make sense of ourselves, others, and the world around us. Perception gives meaning to our experiences. It provides us with the information we use to solve problems and make decisions. It is how we develop our attitudes, formulate our beliefs, and establish our values.

**Perception is more than receiving information,
it includes what we do with that information.**

The perception process includes selection, organization, and interpretation.

1. Selection. Selection is about what information we perceive. We make choices about what is important to us and what is not. There is often more information available to us than we can utilize, so we must select what we feel is useful and filter out the rest. It's a natural process so we generally don't think much about it.

We are more likely to pay attention to things we like or that we find interesting. We select information that fits in with what we already know because it fulfills our expectations reducing uncertainty. We filter out information that is unfamiliar or contradicts what we already know because it can be uncomfortable.

2. Organization. Organization makes information useful to us. It is how we arrange, sort, categorize, and fit together the information we perceive. Information rarely comes in a clearly organized way, so we need to arrange it in a way that's meaningful to us. This makes it easier to recall making it useful to us in the future.

Much of the information we receive comes in bits and pieces. The perception process puts these pieces together, so that we can better understand them. How we organize information fits these pieces together rather like a puzzle. However, this process doesn't always go easily and the puzzle may be missing pieces. So, we have to fill in the missing information, so things make sense.

• The Library. The perception process works like books in a library. Books are organized by topics making it easy for us to find and use them. There is an established method to how they are organized, so that new books can be added whenever they come in and we can find the one we want, when ever we want it.

If the books were put on the shelves in the chronological order they arrived at the library, like how we experience things in life, it would make finding the one we wanted almost impossible. This is why we may need time to process new information, so we can organize our experiences to make them easier to understand and retrieve them when we need them.

3. Interpretation. The law of shared meaning motivates us to make sense out of the information we receive so it can be useful to us. We do this by comparing it to what we already know. Interpretation is based on past experiences, point of view, and social reality. Understanding how we interpret information is essential to understanding how we communicate.

Our past perceptions influence how we make sense of new information. We tend to look for things that are familiar to us because they fit in with the old information more easily. This helps reduce uncertainty and lets us reasonably make assumptions about them. If these perceptions hold true, it can give us confidence to experience new situations.

Interpretation can take time and energy, so when something unexpected or traumatic happens to us we may need time to process the new information. This can be difficult when it challenges what we already know. So, we need to have a way to utilize new information.

We develop our values, attitudes, and opinions from the information we gather through the perception process. Since the media provides much of this information, it can have a significant influence on us. So, it is important to question the validity of the information in the media to be sure that it is true, current, and valid rather than someone's opinion who may be trying to manipulate us.

Knowing how this process works can help us understand why we may have feelings like frustration or anger, so we can better deal with them. Interpretation has the potential to change our perception, which can affect how we communicate with others, our behavior, and how we see ourselves. It is helpful to allow yourself the time to process new information when you need to.

Perception is a skill that can be improved. These techniques can be helpful.

• Reduce uncertainty with feedback. Ask others for feedback to determine how well the messages we communicate to others are received.

• Share meaning by asking questions. Perceptions may be based on inaccurate information, so ask questions to make them more accurate.

• Invest by checking the facts. Opinion and inference are often treated as fact. Check the validity of information for accuracy to make better decisions.

• Be objective. Instead of looking for information to confirm what we already know, look at things from other people's perspectives to learn something new.

• Keep an open mind. This helps us to consider new ideas and learn new things. However, it does not necessarily mean we have to accept them.

• Reduce uncertainty with increased awareness. Be aware of our own assumptions, perspective, and opinions, and how they affect the perception process.

• Things change. Perception helps us reduce uncertainty, but it's important to adapt to change because everything changes. Develop your own ways to adapt the perception process to accommodate new information and changing circumstances.

Expectations.

We have expectations about ourselves, others, and practically everything around us. Without expectations, we could not function in everyday life because they help us to do things without having to think about them. If we had to stop and think about each thing, it would take a lot of time and we would not get very much done.

There are many things that we need to do to get through each day that would not be possible without expectations. For example, we expect to wake up in the morning and go to work. At work we expect to get things done. After work we expect to go home, have dinner, and go to bed.

Our day is full of many of these small expectations. Most of the time they are fulfilled, so we become accustomed to having them met. However, when they don't go as we expect, it can make us feel frustrated or angry. The smaller the expectation, the more we expect it to happen. This can be why people blow up over small, seemingly insignificant things.

**What expectations do you have about yourself,
your family, your job, your coworkers, or your life?**

Think about your perceptions and expectations. Write them down and how well you feel they are being fulfilled. Ask yourself if your expectations are realistic or not. Ask yourself if your perceptions are accurate or not.

Tension, unhappiness, and even conflict can come from inaccurate perceptions and unrealistic expectations. By understanding your perceptions and expectations, you can determine how accurate they are and if they are a source of unnecessary unhappiness. Sometimes clarifying perceptions and expectations can make them more realistic improving your outlook on life.

We want to improve our quality of life, so we expect things to get better over time. If our perceptions don't meet our expectations, it can be frustrating. It can even make us quit trying altogether. If our perceptions exceed our expectations, we may feel that everything is fine and may not do anything to improve ourselves.

To encourage self-improvement, it can be helpful to have expectations that are slightly above your perceptions to motivate yourself to improve. When expectations are slightly above perceptions they are more achievable. If our expectations are too big, it can be discouraging and if they are too small there won't be much improvement.

So, use your perceptions and expectations to motivate your behavior by setting your expectations just enough above your perceptions to motivate you to improve without it becoming discouraging.

Chapter 6
Be More Engaged by Listening

The words listening and hearing are often used interchangeably, however, they are two separate processes that are not the same.

Hearing is receiving sounds, but listening is communicating.

Listening includes perceiving, understanding, organizing, interpreting, remembering, and responding to what we hear. Listening can become second nature, so we don't think about it very much. However, listening is an important skill because it helps us to communicate more effectively.

These are several reasons why listening skills can help us to communicate more effectively with others.

• Time. We spend much of our time communicating and most of that time is listening. Effective listening skills can save us time and energy.
• Information. Listening is how we gain information. The better the information we have, the better decisions we can make.
• Learning. We learn how to do things by listening to others, so we don't have to figure out everything for ourselves.
• Feedback. By listening to feedback we know if our messages are being understood by others, so we can communicate more effectively.
• Growth. By listening we learn about ourselves and the world around us in ways that help facilitate growth.
• Relationships. Listening is essential to creating and maintaining all types of relationships. It is how we learn about others and how they get to know us. Listening shows that we respect and care about others.
• Support. Listening strengthens our relationships by showing others that we support them.
• Likeability. People who listen to others are generally considered more likable because they are seen as considerate of others.
• Career. Listening is an essential skill for our career because it helps us to do our job better. Listening to others who are more experienced can help us improve our skills benefiting our career.
• Self-concept. Listening to others is how we develop our own sense of identity and who we are.
• Awareness. Listening increases our awareness of ourselves, others, and what's going on around us. Increasing awareness makes us more informed and better able to communicate with others.
• Options. Listening to others can provide a source of new ideas giving us more options on how to do things improving our chances of success.

Listening interference.

In the process of communicating, there is the interference of The Great Abyss that prevents our message from getting to others. This interference can also prevent us from listening to what others communicate to us.

Even though we know it's important to listen, there are times when we do not. It's helpful to be aware of the reasons why we don't listen, so that we can make conscious choices about what we listen to and how we listen.

We don't listen because we are unaware that we are not listening.
- Physiological. These are physical impairments that hinder the ability to listen.
- External. This is external noise that is around us which affects how we listen like air conditioners or the traffic outside.
- Prejudgments. We might not listen to things that we feel we have heard before or that have no value to us.
- Wandering. We think faster than we speak, so our mind wanders and we stop listening.
- Overload. There are times when there is too much to listen to, so we block things out.
- Difficult. We are less likely to listen to things that are complex or difficult to understand.
- Unfamiliar. When messages are abstract or unfamiliar, we don't listen because we don't comprehend them.
- Preoccupation. We don't listen because we are thinking about other things that are more interesting or that we need to do.

We don't listen because we have other priorities.
- Time. Listening takes time and we get busy or have more important things to do.
- Effort. Listening takes effort and there are times we don't have the energy to listen.
- Selection. We do not need to listen to everything, so we have to select what we listen to and filter out everything else.
- Interests. We listen to things that we find interesting and filter out things that are boring or that we have heard before.
- Usefulness. We listen to things that we feel will be useful to us or provide a benefit and filter out things that we do not.
- Style. We decide if we are going to listen to something based on the style that the information is presented.

We don't listen because we don't want to listen.
- Critical. We don't listen to information that we do not agree with, approve of, or support.
- Different. We don't listen to things that are a different from what we already know or that challenges what we know.

- Social reality. We don't listen to information that contradicts our perception of social reality because it can be uncomfortable.
- Attitude. We don't listen because we know better or the other person does not know what they are talking about.
- Assumptions. We don't listen because we assume it is not important or we have heard it before.
- Entertainment. We don't listen to things that are not entertaining enough to keep our interest.
- Appearance. We don't listen based on a person's appearance or nonverbal behavior.

We don't listen to avoid people or to get what we want.
- Content. People might act like they are not interested in the topic or what others have to say.
- Value. People might act as if they have nothing to gain, as if what others have to say has no value or benefit to them.
- Domineering. People might try to monopolize or dominate the conversation by talking about themselves.
- Diversions. People might use diversionary tactics like changing the subject to stop others from speaking.
- Defensiveness. People might listen like it's a legal proceeding to gather evidence to defend themselves or to attack others.

Listening Levels of Engagement

We have different expectations of what we hope to gain by listening. Our reasons for listening create levels of engagement. These levels are based on the degree to which we are engaged in what we are listening to based on our desired outcome for listening. Levels of engagement can help us to determine the appropriate approach to use when communicating in various situations.

Level I. Listening for hearing. We listen to background noises around us to tell us information about our surroundings. We listen to traffic sounds, a ringing telephone, or an alarm. This type of listening fulfills our need for information to help us get through the day. Some sounds can warn us of danger. Most of the time this level of listening takes little effort and we do it without thinking much about it.

Level II. Listening for enjoyment. We listen to fulfill our need for enjoyment, relaxation, appreciation, and entertainment. This includes listening to music, the radio, television, or other forms of entertainment. Most of the time we listen passively rather than listening for content or to remember what we heard.

Level III. Listening for awareness. We listen to fulfill our need for information and increase our awareness about what is going on around us. This involves listening to news and information as well as other people.

Level IV. Listening to understand. We listen not only to gain awareness, but also to understand and comprehend the information we hear. We use this type of listening at work and in our relationships.

Level V. Listening to remember. We listen not only to gain and understand information, but also to retain it so that it is useful to us in the future. When we listen to remember, we need to concentrate on what we are hearing and understand it. We may write things down so that we can look at them later to reinforce our memory.

Level VI. Listening to others. We listen to other people's thoughts, feelings, and problems to show that we support them. We change our point of view from our own to the other person's perspective by concentrating on their desired outcome instead of our own. This level of listening helps build relationships by making others feel valued and important.

Level VII. Listening to respond. There are times when people want us to listen and support them without giving them feedback. Other times, they want us to respond to what they have to say. It's important to know the difference because if feedback is given when it is not wanted, it can be perceived as criticism. Our response should be honest, but tactful and considerate of the other person.

Level VIII. Listening to evaluate. We listen not only to understand, but also to evaluate the information we hear. This involves comprehension and analysis to determine the validity of the information we receive. We consider the credibility and motives of the originator of the message to help us from being persuaded to do something we don't want to do.

The listening process.

Listening is a process that is comprised of several stages we go through without thinking much about them. By being aware of how these work, we can listen more effectively. Listening works very similar to the perception process.

1. Hearing. Listening is a physiological process. It is how we receive sound waves transmitted through the air.

2. Receiving. Listening is not only auditory, it is supported by our other senses to complete the message. We hear the words people are saying, but we also see nonverbal behaviors like facial expressions and gestures to tell us how to interpret what we hear.

3. Attention. To listen effectively we need to pay attention to cut through the interference of The Great Abyss. It helps to be aware of our filters and frames of reference that affects what we hear. Messages get through to us depending upon our needs and wants, interests, and desired outcomes. This part of the process is motivated by the law of uncertainty to reduce uncertainty.

4. Selection. We select information by evaluating what we hear to determine its usefulness because we cannot possibly listen to or use everything we might hear. Selection is when we choose what we will listen to and what we will ignore. It is based upon our needs, wants, and desired outcomes.

5. Organization. When we listen, information does not necessarily come in any particular order. It can seem chaotic, coming in random bits and pieces that we need to organize into recognizable patterns so we can understand and use them. If it fits in with something we already know, it is more easily understood. Organization makes information easier to recall, so it can be more useful to us in the future.

6. Understanding. In order for information to be useful to us, we need to give it meaning. We are motivated to do this by the law of shared meaning. We make sense of the information we hear by comparing it to our past knowledge. If it does not fit in with what we know, we may discard it.

7. Interpreting. By interpreting information we give it meaning beyond what is actually contained in the message. We use it to draw conclusions and determine what it means for us. This is why even when people have the same information, they might interpret it differently based on their own individual perspectives.

8. Remembering. Information is more useful to us when we are able to recall it at a later time. We tend to remember only about half of what we hear, and after a while only about half of that. We can utilize techniques to help us remember information like acronyms, mnemonics, and other word tricks or by taking notes. Remembering makes information useful to us long after we have received it. The more important and useful information is to us, the more likely we are to remember it.

9. Responding. Responding shows consideration for other people and provides them with feedback. We respond by asking questions and relating our own experiences. It can be both verbal, using expressions like yes or no, and nonverbal, using eye contact, head nodding, and facial expressions like smiling. Responding provides feedback to show support. If we do not respond it can be perceived as rejection.

Listening Skills

We assume that everyone knows how to listen because we may think that it doesn't take any particular skill. Listening skills are like other communicating skills that can be developed and improved.

These are some options to help develop effective listening skills.

• Consider the desired outcome of others. When you listen to someone consider their desired outcome or purpose for speaking. Do they want help, to share information, persuade you, or self-disclose? By understanding their desired outcome, you can avoid misunderstandings that can make communicating more difficult. If it is not clear, ask them to tactfully draw them out.

• Consider your desired outcome. We listen to others for a reason, so what is your reason for listening? Knowing why you are listening to others helps you to know what to listen for and how to listen.

• Work together. Listening involves both people working together, rather than competing to see who gets their way. Looking for common ground shows that you are considerate of their point of view. This does not necessarily mean you have to agree with them.

• Time. Find a time when you have enough time to listen. Avoid times when people are in a bad mood or are rushed. Have a definite ending time so the other person focuses on what's important and things don't go on indefinitely.

• Place. Avoid discussing important issues in an inappropriate place like in public or in front of others. Having a place to listen that is comfortable and free of distractions helps you to focus your attention on what they have to say. The best place is a room free of noise, that is comfortable, and provides privacy.

• Respond. Providing feedback and appropriate responses shows that you are interested in what they have to say. Respond by saying yes and smiling or nodding. Ask open ended questions to draw them out, because people do not always say what they mean. Let the other person have their say before responding.

• Emotions. People may want us to listen so they can express their feelings and emotions. It's easy to absorb their emotions as our own, so we might respond with the same emotional intensity. Stay calm, don't tell them how they should be feeling, and don't characterize their feelings as right or wrong.

We want to tell them they shouldn't feel bad because we care about them. However, this can make things worse because it discounts how they feel. If it seems like they are getting mad at you chances are it's not really about you.

Reasoning

Reasoning can help you evaluate
information, solve problems, and make decisions.

Reasoning is using an established set of rules to make an argument or come to a conclusion. It is how we organize information so others can better understand it. It is the basis or premise for our ideas. It is the means we use to persuade others. Analytical reasoning helps us analyze and evaluate ideas or the claims other people make. We use reasoning to improve the effectiveness of how we communicate with others.

Reasoning consists of the following elements.

1. Rules. Analytical reasoning utilizes a set of rules and methods for obtaining and analyzing information to reach a conclusion. The purpose is to set aside personal preferences to discover the truth. For example, our judicial system uses analytical reasoning and an established set of procedural rules and laws that govern the process of presenting and utilizing evidence in a court of law to make a determination of guilt or innocence.

2. Claim. Reasoning begins with a claim you want to prove. For example, a lawyer wants to prove that their client is innocent. A claim asserts what facts are relevant to the case and what evidence can be used. It can determine values like whether something is right or wrong, good or bad.

3. Criteria. We hear people making claims about all kinds of things every day. Instead of using objective criteria to make a claim, people may present their own opinions as fact. Analytical reasoning utilizes clearly defined criteria that consists of a pre-established means to evaluate the claim. For example, criteria to evaluate a new building might include energy efficiency or cost effectiveness. The criteria must be universally recognized, objective, and based on the evidence instead of on opinion or emotion.

4. Evidence. Information must be presented to support a claim and its validity or truthfulness. Evidence can include facts, statistics, illustrations, observation, experience, comparisons, descriptions, and expert or individual testimony. Evidence needs to be accurate and objective, it must stand up to scrutiny, and be based on fact rather than inference or personal opinion. It can be evaluated using established criteria to determine its validity and credibility. It should be clear, easily understood, and support the claim, otherwise it may undermine the argument. Building an argument is like building a wall with evidence as the bricks and reasoning as the mortar to hold them together.

5. Source. In order to evaluate the claim, the source of the information should be evaluated using the same criteria. Information does not simply just exist on its own, it must come from somewhere and where it comes from can make a difference. A source should be trustworthy and credible, honest and reliable. There are many types of sources like research institutions, associations, universities, government, companies, organizations, groups, and individuals. The credibility of a source can come from expertise, experience, education, training, credentials, and reputation. Knowing the source is important because more credible sources usually provide better information.

6. Organization. This is the order in which evidence is presented to support a claim. It involves what information is selected to use and how it is presented. We can use different methods of organization to help find solutions to problems, as well as determine their causes. Several methods are described in this book.

7. Findings. The purpose of this process is to establish findings that support the claim. The findings include a conclusion or summary of your argument. It includes new knowledge that has been gained in the process. It can be used to determine if the initial claim is true or false. For example, evidence that is presented in a court trial uses reasoning to reach a finding of guilt or innocence. However, most of the time findings are not as straightforward.

Fallacies.

Flaws in reasoning are called fallacies and increasing your awareness of how they are used can help you to avoid using them in the arguments you make and in evaluating the claims other people make.

• False evidence. Evidence may be distorted, faulty, or personal opinion.

• False generalizations. Making generalizations based on too few examples that are not applicable to a larger group.

• False crisis. People can be motivated by crisis and a fabricated crisis can motivate people to do things they would not otherwise do.

• False history. You may hear someone say, "This is the way we've always done it." They are claiming that doing something for a while makes it valid. Because times change, what has been done in the past may not be valid today.

• False analogy. Analogies compare two things to transfer the characteristics of one to another. A false analogy compares two things that are not similar.

• False causation. Claiming that one event causes another or that a series of events will conclude in a specific result without establishing that there are any actual relationships between them.

• False connection. Making a claim that does not follow from its basic premise by creating a connection when none exists. Organizing evidence in a way that is not consistent with established methods of organization.

• False choice. Presenting a choice between several possibilities knowing that all except one are undesirable or unworkable. Or presenting several choices that are just restatements of the same thing.

• False authority. Utilizing someone who is not an authority or expert. A common approach is using a celebrity in place of expertise or credibility.

• False conclusion. Presenting valid information and reasoning that does not support the findings or conclusions.

• Missing information. Presenting only the portion of the information that supports the claim while leaving out other information that discredits it.

• Diversion. Creating a false issue to divert people's attention from another issue. When an argument doesn't have merit on its own, another more pressing argument diverts people's attention, so they don't examine the first argument as closely.

• Circular reasoning. Presenting a claim as its own findings without offering supporting evidence. This reasoning goes in a circle because the claim is used as its own evidence.

• Ambiguity. Purposeful ambiguity is being unclear in order to confuse others so they won't follow your reasoning. This can be done by using language that is overly technical, ambiguous, or confusing so that flaws won't be noticed.

• Incomplete. This approach is used when only parts of an argument hold true. It is used when an entire argument or claim does not have validity or enough evidence to support it.

• Emotion. Rather than appealing to reasoning or evidence, this approach uses emotional appeals to motivate people to take action. Some of the most effective appeal to fear, anger, sympathy, nostalgia, or guilt.

• Assumptions. Much of what we do is based on assumptions. We could not function if we had to question everything we do every day. However, assumptions are all too often treated as facts or evidence. It is common to take one assumption and then pile on another and another until they are taken as fact. When one of the arguments does not hold true, everything falls apart.

• Accusations. If an opponent cannot discredit a person's argument, they may attack the person so others will not listen to their argument or anything else they may say. While source credibility is important, an argument may still have validity and should be evaluated on its own merit.

• Repetition makes right. This is a common method of utilizing repetition of information in place of reasoning. Information is repeated over and over until it begins to take on a validity of its own.

• Correlation used as causation. This is a commonly used fallacy where people claim that one event is the cause of another when they only exist at the same time. A correlation is when two or more things have an interdependent relationship or they occur simultaneously. Causation is when one event or action causes another by having a direct effect on it.

Chapter 7
Be Better-Looking Using Verbal and Nonverbal Skills

Language is the system of spoken and written words we use to communicate with one another. It is a means of communicating where symbols are invested with meaning and shared by groups of people. In order for language to work, everyone has to agree on what the symbols mean and how to use them.

Language is something all people have in common, but all people do not share a common language. Different groups of people have developed their own specialized ways of communicating based upon their ethnicity, culture, profession, or geographic affiliation.

The advantage of language is in its ability to convert everything we know and experience into symbols that can be easily shared by large numbers of people. It gives us the ability to share, store, and transmit large quantities of information relatively easily. The power of language is in its ability to affect how we think and how it motivates our behavior. How we use language can help others to perceive us as confident, likable, professional, attractive, perhaps even better-looking.

Language enables us to work with one another to accomplish things and achieve our desired outcomes. It is the means by which we define ourselves, others, and everything around us. It is how we learn about and make sense of ourselves and the world around us. Without language, life as we know it would not be possible.

**Language is about making choices
and the choices we make communicate who we are
as a person and how we want to be perceived by others.**

Language allows us to do many things that could not be done without it.
* Language takes symbols and invests them with meaning.
* Language is how we share information and ideas.
* Language is how we share our experiences, creating common culture.
* Language is how we make connections with others.
* Language shapes who we are as a person, our self-concept, and our identity.
* Language helps us to create and maintain relationships.
* Language can create and change perceptions and expectations.
* Language is how we make our ideas a reality.
* Language helps us to measure things and communicates their value.
* Language tells us what is important, what we value, and what we don't.
* Language creates historical, social, cultural, and monetary value.
* Language makes judgments by describing things as good or bad, rare or common, and expensive or cheap.
* Language helps us to have power and control over resources and people.

- Language is how we create and enforce the rules of society.
- Language shapes our perception of nationality, ethnicity, and culture.
- Language is how we make sense of ourselves, others, and the world around us.
- Language fulfills our need to express ourselves artistically and creatively.
- Language can create and share emotions or inspire us.
- Language can engage our minds and touch our hearts.

If you think language is no big deal,
try communicating using only pictures, drawings, or gestures for a day.

We use these different types of language when we communicate.
- The formal form of English, based upon British English.
- The more commonly used form of a language. Standard American English is the common form of English spoken primarily in the United States, as well as in other countries.
- Vernacular. The ordinary, everyday spoken language that reflects how language is commonly used.
- Colloquialisms. Informal words and phrases used in conversation.
- Slang. Shorthand references to communicate more complex concepts that reflect current culture.
- Dialect. Regional or local variations of language that reflects its history or culture.
- Grammar. The formal rules that govern how language is used.
- Semantics. This is how meaning is created in language through use.
- Syntax. How words are organized in order to communicate, as some words have different meanings based upon word order.
- Jargon. Specialized technical language and terms used by professions to increase precision and accuracy in communicating.
- Denotative language. Language that has literal common dictionary definitions. A word denotes its meaning.
- Connotative language. The words carry additional implied meanings beyond their literal dictionary definition.

In the process of communicating, you create your Great Idea and make connections with others who receive your message and hopefully understand it. However, interference can change the meaning of your Great Idea, so that it is not clearly understood by others.

In order to communicate more effectively, it's helpful to have an awareness of the following potential problems with language to avoid them.

• Ambiguity. This is a lack of clarity that creates confusion about what you say. Increasing uncertainty about your message can happen by not being specific or using words that can be interpreted in more than one way. It can be overcome by being specific and using precise language.

• Vagueness. This is not being specific about what we say or mean. It can be intentional or unintentional. We may be vague intentionally, so we do not offend others or to protect their feelings. This can be overcome through clarity, using precise language, and soliciting feedback.

• Interpretation. We may not be aware of how others interpret what we say. This can be overcome by using easily understood language and clarifying our message by soliciting feedback.

• Multiple meanings. There are words that have similar or multiple meanings that could cause confusion. We can clarify what we mean through explanations or by understanding the context in which they are used.

• Comparative language. These are words that only have meaning in comparison to something else. This includes words like larger, smaller, faster, slower, above, below, later, or earlier. Understanding what these words mean relies on knowing the basis for comparison. Using definite and precise language like numerical references can make these meanings clear.

• Euphemisms. We use euphemisms to protect people's feelings because they can be more socially acceptable. However, they can be perceived as not being straightforward. A better approach is to avoid using them by being truthful, but tactful.

• Abstract language. We use this type of language to describe things, ideas, and concepts that are new or do not physically exist. Abstract language can be clarified by comparing the unfamiliar to something that is familiar.

• Clichés. We use these phrases to substitute for what we really want to say because they don't take much thought or effort. Instead, think about what you really want to say and then say that.

• Addictive language. It is easy to get into the habit of using words that have no meaning including like, yet, you know, kind of, or I guess. Using them can undermine the effectiveness of what you have to say. Instead, say what you mean and cut these out.

• Throwaway language. We can get into the habit of using modifiers that have no meaning. These include words like literally, very, actually, or whatever. Sometimes they are useful, but most of the time you can do without them. You can tell if a word is necessary by removing it and if the meaning doesn't change, don't use it.

These are language skills to help you communicate more effectively.
•   Use language that is plain, clear, and easy to understand.
•   Use the language of your audience, so they will understand you.
•   Use language appropriate for your audience's understanding of the topic.
•   Use language correctly and accurately to avoid misunderstandings.

- Use language that is familiar. When talking about the unfamiliar, connect it to something people already know.
- Use language that describes events as if they are happening in the present to make them more interesting.
- Use language that appeals to the five senses. Let people know how things look, sound, feel, taste, or smell to make your message more real.
- Use precise language by choosing the right word and using it correctly.
- Use modifiers sparingly such as actually, very, or literally.
- Use language without fillers such as like, yeah, whatever, or you know.
- Use imagery to create a picture in the mind of your audience to help them understand and remember your idea.
- Use examples and illustrations to clarify ideas by including experiences and situations people find familiar.
- Use emotional language to make a connection with people, so your message is more engaging.

• But. The word "but" can cancel out everything that has been said up to it, by substituting what is said after it. For example, in a relationship a person might say, "You're a wonderful person, but I think we should just be friends." The bottom line is the relationship is over.

• Personal pronouns. When we use the word "I" we take responsibility for ourselves. We might use the pronoun "you" to blame or shift responsibility to others. When we use the words "we" or "us" it creates a connection with others. The word "they" often refers to people we don't know. These words can be used as a way to include or exclude other people.

• Directive language. We use this language to give directions how to get somewhere like driving directions, how to do something, or how something works. Use visual information to help them understand what you describe. Give people the big picture so they know how everything fits together. Give them the beginning and ending points for reference, where they begin, and what things look like at the end. Use common terms and be consistent using them. For example, in giving directions use north-south, left-right, or inches and feet depending upon your purpose.

Use familiar markers to let people know where they are, where they have been, and where they are going. This is so everybody is in the same spot because it's easy to get lost on the way. Let people know potential problems like where they might get lost or go the wrong direction.

Nonverbal Communicating

Verbal communicating consists of both spoken and written language, so nonverbal communicating consists of practically everything else. While it is not the words we speak, it does include how we say them. It includes our facial expressions, body language, and appearance.

We communicate information nonverbally by how we look, how we act, and how we use our time, space, and money. Practically everything we create, have around us, and everything we do has the potential to communicate nonverbally.

If it communicates something to others and does not use words, it can be considered nonverbal communicating.

We are motivated to look at other people's nonverbal behavior because we don't intentionally communicate nonverbally the same way we intentionally communicate verbally.

We tend to give nonverbal behavior more significance than what people say because it is considered more genuine.

Our nonverbal behavior communicates information in addition to the message that we send to others. So, in order to communicate more effectively, it can be helpful to be aware of how nonverbal communicating can affect us.

- Nonverbal information can support a message giving it additional meaning. We might gesture, point, or pound our fist to emphasize what we are saying.
- Nonverbal information can substitute for verbal information by replacing what we might say verbally like nodding yes or shaking our head no.
- Nonverbal information can contradict verbal information when we don't say what we mean or when we don't want to talk.
- Nonverbal information can hide the message when we don't want others to know what we think or feel. We might use it to cover our true feelings.

Nonverbal behavior can communicate the nature of a relationship between people. We can use it to observe others in order to understand their relationships. These are some relationships that can be communicated nonverbally.

• Authority. People in positions of authority use nonverbal behavior like direct eye contact, posture, close proximity, and the loudness of their voice to assert their authority. They may use their voice, distance, stance, posture, and eye contact to assert dominance, status, prestige, and power over others.

• Affiliation. Relationships are expressed through nonverbal behavior. People communicate warmth, closeness, friendship, and intimacy through eye contact, the tone of their voice, touch, and facial expressions.

• Attraction. We can be attracted to others by their nonverbal behavior. We respond to positive eye contact, close proximity, facial expressions like smiling, and touch as a sign of attraction. Attraction can vary from professional to personal. We may be attracted to work with people who act professional or to form friendships with people we enjoy being around.

Voice

How you say the words you speak is considered nonverbal characteristics. This is the extra information we add to our words that tells others how to interpret what we say. We rarely speak without adding additional nonverbal information. If we didn't, we would speak in a monotone voice.

These are some vocal characteristics to be aware of because they affect how people interpret what you say.

• Pitch. This is the high or low tone of your voice, which can be similar to the notes on a musical scale. If we are nervous or stressed our voice tends to have a higher pitch. If we don't want people to know we are nervous, we can consciously lower the tone of our voice to sound more confident.

• Volume. This is how loud or soft we speak. When we are angry we might let people know by speaking loudly or shouting at them. If something is more personal we might speak softly to emphasize privacy.

• Pacing. This is how fast or slow we speak. If we aren't sure what to say we may speak slower. If we are nervous we might speak faster. If we feel nervous and don't want others to know, we can speak at a more average pace.

• Inflection. These are the changes we make in the intonation or sound of our voice in order to emphasize important points or to differentiate between different topics.

• Timbre. This is the quality or fullness of our voice. Sometimes we speak with a full resonant voice and other times we may have a nasal or airy quality. We convey emotion through the timbre of our voice like when it cracks or waivers with emotion. It can sound rich, energetic, or lively. Or, it can sound thin, flat, nasal, or raspy. When we speak more resonant we sound more confident.

• Pronunciation. This is correctly saying the words we speak. Articulation is speaking clearly so that other people can understand us.

• Vocal variation. Combining several vocal elements together creates variety. This helps to cut through the interference of The Great Abyss. Vocal variation adds interest so that others are more likely to listen to what we have to say. Variation is a matter of balance. Too much vocal variation can be annoying making us difficult to listen to and too little makes us sound monotonous or boring.

• Pauses. What you don't say can be as significant as what you do say. Pauses are like breaks between paragraphs or chapters on a written page. They highlight important points, transitions, and give people time to think about what you said. We use a dramatic pause for effect before and after a significant word or phrase to set it apart, like using boldface type or an exclamation mark on a written page.

• Silence. This can communicate many things. Silence can be uncomfortable, pressuring us to say something. It can be considered rude or an expression of anger or rejection. We may have a moment of silence to show respect or reverence. It can express emotions. It's what we might do when we don't know what to say. The meaning of silence is based upon the context of the situation and the people involved because it can have many interpretations.

Body Language

Body language refers to how we use our body to communicate with others. It is a form of nonverbal communicating that we not only use to support the words we say, but also to communicate information without saying anything.

Body language includes our appearance like our posture, demeanor, and bearing. It includes how we move parts of our body like our head, arms, hands, and legs. It includes gestures, facial expressions, and eye contact. It provides information that shapes our perception of others. Much of what we perceive about others we learn by observing their behavior, which helps us to form expectations about them.

**How we use body language to communicate nonverbally
can help others to perceive us as better-looking.**

These are several functions that nonverbal body language fulfills.

• First impressions. When we first meet someone we use the perception process to form an impression of them based upon their nonverbal body language. We reduce uncertainty by observing a person's appearance, demeanor, mannerisms, and how they speak because we generally don't have much other information. While first impressions can be inaccurate, they can be difficult to change once formed.

• Likeability. When we meet someone, we want to like them and want them to like us. We rarely meet people we want to dislike nor do we want people to dislike us. We perceive people as likable based upon their nonverbal body language. For example, we can be perceived as more likable if we smile, lean slightly towards others, make appropriate eye contact, and shake hands. People can be perceived as distant if they avoid eye contact, don't smile, or have little movement.

• Balance. We feel comfortable with balanced nonverbal behavior that is not too extreme. For example, people who speak with a slightly lower pitch, even pacing, and vocal variety can be perceived as more confident than those who have a high pitch, fast pacing, and uneven intonation. Too little eye contact can make others uncomfortable as well as having too much eye contact. To find the right balance, we use self awareness and feedback to determine how we are being perceived.

• Feedback. We use the nonverbal behavior of others as a kind of feedback to let us know how we are coming across to them. Positive feedback includes a smile, nod, or leaning forward. The nonverbal feedback others provide lets us know how they perceive us, which can affect the future of the relationship.

• Credibility. Much of what we perceive as credible is communicated nonverbally through body language and appearance. People are perceived as credible when they make appropriate eye contact, have proper posture, speak with a clear voice, use even pacing, have proper pronunciation, and speak clearly because these things reduce uncertainty.

People can be perceived as less credible if they don't make eye contact, look around or at the ground, have poor posture, shift from side to side, speak with a high pitch, use rapid pacing, or don't pronounce words properly or enunciate clearly.

• Control. We use nonverbal behavior to communicate control, dominance, or authority over others. Standing in close proximity, lowering the pitch of our voice, speaking louder, and steady pacing can give the perception of authority. Using extreme eye contact can he perceived as exerting dominance or intensity.

People may be perceived as being submissive if they avoid eye contact, speak in a low volume or tone, shift their posture, or move away. However, what is perceived as submissiveness could actually be nervousness or being uncomfortable because of the mannerisms of others.

• Aggressiveness. People may use nonverbal techniques to pressure others to get them to do what they want them to do. By understanding how nonverbal body language works you can protect yourself from this. If someone is pressuring you by being aggressive, you can protect yourself without escalating the situation. Remain calm, but confident. Speak slowly in a clear, firm voice to assert yourself.

Elements of nonverbal body language.

• Posture. One of the first things people notice about others is their posture. They make judgments based upon how a person stands and how they move. This includes their posture, stature, and bearing. Good posture involves standing with your back straight, shoulders back, head up, with your feet about the same distance apart as your shoulders. Bearing is the way a person moves or stands. Having good bearing means that you move at a steady pace with confidence, avoiding sudden or jerky movements.

We often perceive people with good posture as competent, educated, likable, and as having a positive attitude. People who slouch, lean against walls, shift their feet, or have rounded shoulders can be perceived as sloppy, untrustworthy, incompetent, or having a low self-concept. People make judgments about our posture because it can be perceived as a reflection of our pride and confidence in ourselves.

• Gestures. We gesture by moving parts of our body including our hands, arms, fingers, head, legs, and feet. Gestures are used to emphasize words and phrases. They add interest to what we say. We can use gestures in place of words like when we wave hello or goodbye. They can be used to express feelings and emotions. They are used to show directions or demonstrate how something works. Gestures can be deliberate, however, we often use them without thinking or out of habit.

Gestures should look natural, be used sparingly and appropriately. People who use gestures can be seen as more interesting and engaging because they give the impression of being confident and likable. People who do not use gestures can be perceived as withdrawn or not interested in others.

Excessive gesturing can be perceived as being nervous, lacking confidence, or even aggression. Being aware of how gestures are perceived helps improve communicating skills so that we are perceived as being more self assured and confident.

• Facial expressions. Our face is the most noticed and expressive part of our body. It is our most distinctive and individually unique characteristic. Facial expressions include our eyes, mouth, lips, chin, forehead, and eyebrows. While many of our facial expressions are intentional, others can be involuntary based upon what we are saying, thinking, or feeling. We are motivated by the law of uncertainty to look for meaning in facial expressions to provide us information about others.

We tend to trust facial expressions more than words because they are perceived to be more honest since they are spontaneous, even though sometimes people might try to use them to their advantage. Most of the time we use facial expressions to support what we are saying, however, we also use them in other ways.

We can make what we say more intense, like when we are surprised. We can minimize our reactions to show that something doesn't bother us. We might cover up our expressions to hide what we are thinking or feeling. Or we can use expressions that have little or no meaning so others won't know how we really feel.

• Eye contact. There's an old adage that says the eyes are the window to the soul. Our eyes can be used to express emotions like sympathy, surprise, affection, intimacy, or anger. We look into people's eyes to determine if they are telling the truth, their motivation, their credibility, or how they are feeling. We use eye contact to express affection or intimacy, to emphasize important points, or to threaten others.

We use eye contact to get people's attention to make a connection or to discourage them by turning away. When we speak to a group of people we make eye contact to create a connection with them. We interpret how others look at us when we are speaking as feedback to let us know how we are coming across to them.

Chapter 8
Be Happier Expressing Emotions

Emotions are the psychological and physiological responses to our experiences, perceptions, and expectations. They are often spontaneous reactions to our interactions with others or our own thoughts. They can affect how we communicate with others. They can motivate our behavior and actions. They can help or hurt our self-concept. They are an unavoidable and inevitable part of life that can make it fun and exciting, or sad and overwhelming.

Sometimes we feel emotions that we would rather not feel. We may feel that we have little control over our emotions. By understanding how emotions can be a nonverbal expression of our thoughts and feelings, we can utilize them to communicate more effectively with others. Understanding our emotions helps us to better understand ourselves. While we can't always control how we feel, we can have more control over how our emotions affect us.

Be aware of how the following circumstances can affect our emotions.

• Extreme emotions. These emotions can come on all of a sudden or they can build up over time. We may get carried away in the heat of the moment and end up saying or doing things we do not intend to do. We may react instinctively to defend ourselves escalating the situation. We might do this out of a need to protect ourselves. It's helpful to get in the habit of understanding our emotions because of the potential impact they have on us and on others.

• Multiple emotions. Things can happen that cause us to feel several emotions at the same time. Sometimes they can be positive like feeling happy and excited. However, when they are conflicted it can be a source of tension or unhappiness. For instance, someone we know may land a great job, get married, or have a baby. If these are things that we want, but don't have, we can be happy for them while also being upset they haven't happened to us. This can make us feel conflicted creating tension because we want them to be happy, but we want to be happy too.

• Past emotions. We all have had past experiences where we felt strong emotions. While that was in the past, we can have new experiences that make us feel the same emotions. For instance, we might have had a relationship end badly that left us feeling sad or angry. Some time later, we might have another relationship end and under other circumstances, we would feel bad for only a short time.

However, because of our past experience, we have a recurrence of the emotions from the past making this breakup more intense. The effects of emotions can accumulate over time, so if similar situations keep reoccurring, emotional feelings can become more intense.

• Negative emotions. We tend to remember negative emotions longer because they can be stronger. They represent something that is unresolved making them uncomfortable, so we spend time thinking about what we could have done about them. They can change our physiology like our pulse or blood pressure. We are more likely to do something when we feel negative emotions because they are uncomfortable.

We might even do things that under other less extreme circumstances we would not do. It can be helpful to have an awareness of how negative emotions affect our behavior to avoid making things worse. Strong emotions can be a very powerful motivator. One of the most effective ways to motivate people is to make them fearful or angry.

• Defensiveness. In a disagreement or conflict, the emotional intensity can easily escalate. We want to defend ourselves from what we see as a potential threat. For example, if someone is angry we may become angry to defend ourselves. We may feel that we have to match their emotional intensity in order to get through to them, so if they yell we might yell back.

We should never become angry just because someone else is angry because it can make things worse. In order to defuse the situation, stay calm and in touch with your own emotions by considering your desired outcome. Ask yourself, do you want to resolve the problem or make it worse?

• Emotional control. Emotions can motivate us to say and do things we would not do under other circumstances or they can paralyze us so we do nothing. This can be a problem unless we do something to control them. While we cannot control how we feel, being aware of our emotions can help us to know what we are communicating to others and how they perceive us.

If you are in an emotional situation,
take a moment to consider your desired outcome.

Doing this can help you to not let circumstances control you. It can stop the emotional momentum giving you time to consider your options to stay in control, so you can choose the best approach for the situation.

Expressing emotions.

In order to deal with our emotions it's helpful to be aware of what they really are. All too often if someone asks us how we are feeling we simply say, "I'm fine." We might have difficulty expressing or even understanding our emotions, so these are some methods to help increase your awareness of your emotions.

Reduce uncertainty by increasing your awareness of what causes your emotions. What things motivate which emotions? What makes you feel good or happy?

What makes you upset or depressed? Awareness helps you make good choices about what to do. If you know the source of negative emotions, you can reduce your contact with them. You can do more things that make you feel good and spend time with people who are positive.

While it is not always possible to avoid negativity all the time, having an increased awareness can make us more prepared for dealing with bad situations and keep us from absorbing the emotions of others.

Consider how we share meaning with emotions. When someone experiences extreme emotions we have a natural tendency to tell them to relax. This can make them more upset because people do not like to be told what to do.

It discounts how they are feeling by implying that their emotions do not matter. Instead, ask them about their emotions and why they are feeling the way they do. They may simply want someone to listen.

Invest in relationships by talking with someone. We tend to hide our emotions from others, even from ourselves. We may act happy when in reality we are not. We do this because people prefer to be around others who are happy and upbeat.

It can be helpful to find someone we trust to talk to about our feelings. This can make us feel better because it relieves stress and reduces tension by getting it out of our system to help us feel better.

Know your desired outcome. Determine who you can talk to about how you feel. Choose an appropriate time and place to talk so they will feel comfortable listening. Let them know why you want to talk about your feelings. Do you want to vent, have them support you, give you feedback, or do something?

While it can be good to be honest about how you feel, the reality is that not all emotions should be shared, especially if they could be hurtful to others. It's always good to be tactful to see how they are accepted because not everyone will accept all types of feelings, especially if they are about them.

Decide to be happy. Given a choice between feeling good or bad, which would you choose? While we cannot turn our emotions on and off it's helpful to be aware of what makes us upset, so we can do more to be happy. Emotions come from our state of mind, so if our state of mind can make us upset, it should also be able to make us happy.

By doing this, we take something bad and turn it around to make it better. There are times when that is not so easy because other people do things that make us upset. But if someone does something bad to us why should we feel bad about it, because they probably don't feel bad about it. Feeling bad does not make anything better for you.

Be realistic by checking your perceptions and expectations to see if they are accurate. We may feel emotions based upon faulty perceptions or unrealistic expectations. Things are often not as bad as they seem, so being aware of what causes emotions can help you prepare for them and know what to do when they happen.

Choose an appropriate time and place to express your emotions. Most of the time we express our emotions when we feel them without thinking about the consequences. This is because emotions can happen without warning so we respond right away when it may be better to wait until later.

While it is generally good to be honest about our emotions, the reality is that there are times when we should not let others know how we feel. By expressing our emotions in the heat of the moment we may say things we don't mean. It's better to choose a time and place when others would be more receptive to them.

It's helpful to keep emotions, even negative ones, in a positive light. For example, rather than saying, "You made me angry," you might say, "When this happens, I feel angry." Sharing emotions follows the rules of self-disclosure because sharing information about ourselves can build trust, however, it should be done incrementally and appropriately. It can be helpful for others to share their experiences, but it should not become a contest to see who has had it the worst.

Emotions come from our state of mind, so if our state of mind can make us upset, it should also be able to make us feel happier.

Stress Management

Stress is an inevitable and unavoidable part of our lives caused by unresolved tension. It is an emotional and physiological expression of uncertainty that can come from unresolved problems, decisions, or unfulfilled needs and wants.

Tension and stress can lead to medical problems, but if kept to a reasonable level it can be helpful because it can give us a boost of energy when we need it. It can heighten our perception and motivate us to take action.

By increasing our awareness we can look at what causes stress because we may have the perception that something is stressful when the stress may be coming from somewhere else. While we cannot totally alleviate stress, having an awareness of its sources and effects makes it easier for us to do something about it.

These are some options to help manage stress.

• Reduce uncertainty by communicating. When faced with a stressful situation, we may react in a way that can make the stress worse. How we communicate in times of stress can determine how we feel about it. It's helpful to communicate in a clear, accurate, and positive way that will help you to cope with stress.

Communicating in negative, unrealistic, and confusing ways can make the situation worse and more stressful. While that may sound obvious, we can have a natural tendency to make things worse because it's easy to do.

Identifying the source and scope of the stress, coming up with options to deal with it, and then following through can be a more difficult, but more effective approach.

• Awareness can help give us a realistic perspective on the problem. It can help us determine what is causing stress and how it's affecting us. It can help us choose the best approach to resolve stress. Having options gives us a variety of ways to choose the best one for success. These can be prepared ahead of time, so when you feel stress you can do something about it.

• Confidence helps us to stay in control of the situation, to focus on the problem, and to evaluate our options. It helps to have realistic perceptions and expectations about what we can do. We can improve our confidence by developing a plan for stressful situations. Confidence comes from experience and belief in our own abilities. By preparing for stressful situations, we can be more confident when they occur.

• Competence. Since stress is a natural part of life, we can be prepared for things we know will happen that are stressful. We know that we might face stressful situations like medical issues, work problems, and financial difficulties. We know that life can be unpredictable, so we can prepare for things like accidents, acts of nature, or illness. We can reduce stress when we have the confidence that we are prepared to handle stressful situations.

• Be positive. While it sounds cliché, it helps to remain positive during stressful situations. This helps us to concentrate on the issue at hand. Be positive, but truthful and realistic. Don't make assumptions or jump to conclusions that could cause unnecessary stress. Show confidence by using positive facial expressions, open posture, self assured gestures, and definite movements.

Lack of confidence can be communicated through nonverbal behaviors like confusing facial expressions, excessive gestures, fidgeting, pacing back and forth, or tugging on hair or clothing. If you act confident others should pick up on your confidence and are more likely to reflect it back to you, making you feel more confident about yourself.

Anger Management

Despite our best intentions, situations can escalate beyond our capacity to handle them. Feelings of frustration can turn to conflict and anger. Once this happens it may be difficult to stop. Anger is often the result of conflicts going unresolved due to uncertainty. Anger is an emotion that is communicated to get attention or to motivate others to fulfill a specific desired outcome.

Expressing anger can provide emotional release for the moment, but it can have unintended and undesirable outcomes. It can lead to defensiveness and provoke retaliation from others.

Anger can damage your health by contributing to higher blood pressure, a weakened immunity to illness, and increased levels of cortical that could increase the potential for artery blockage or heart attack.

People don't like to be around others who are angry
whether they are right or not.

It can be helpful to use the following options to help reduce anger.
- Identify the real issues. We can get angry before actually understanding the issues and scope of the problem.
- Identify the source. Knowing what causes feelings of anger can help you to better deal with them.
- Consider the potential consequences. Consider what it might do to your relationships with others and what it could do to you.
- Distance yourself from the source of the anger. Avoid people and situations that create anger when possible.
- Make changes to avoid repeating circumstances that could create anger.
- Look at what you know in a new way to change the things that make you angry.
- Consider avoiding or eliminating situations and relationships that cause anger.
- Get support from people you feel comfortable talking with and who you trust.

Anger can come from feelings of fear. Fear is an emotional response to heightened uncertainty that can have tangible consequences. By increasing our awareness, we can put our fears into perspective, so they don't have as much control over us.

We are told to face our fears, but fear can be good because it can protect us from harm. Fear can be like a smoke detector. We should not try to disable it, but instead understand how it can help us and what to do when is sounds an alarm.

You might tell someone you trust about your feelings to release built up emotions. They may have been in similar situations and have had similar feelings. Hearing about their experiences may help you to better cope with your feelings.

When you feel angry stop and ask yourself, what is your desired outcome? This may provide a moment to defuse the situation preventing it from escalating. Rarely is our desired outcome to get angry with someone, yell at them, retaliate, or make an enemy out of them.

If someone is angry at us and we do not respond in anger, if they are still angry then that's their problem. If we respond angrily, then it has become our problem. It's not that we don't want to get angry, it's just that it usually doesn't do any good.

Chapter 9
Be Smarter with Your Space, Time, and Money

Space Management

Space consists of everything that is around us. There are many types of space and there are many ways that we utilize it. Space may have been created by nature, but people have developed many ways to divide and change it to fulfill their needs and wants.

We have physical spaces we occupy like where we live and work, including our homes and workplaces. We create emotional space in our relationships with others. We have space that we seek to control such as areas of influence and expertise like our turf or territory.

The spaces that we inhabit nonverbally communicate information about us to others. Our own personal space communicates information to others nonverbally because of the choices we make and what it reveals about us. We often inhabit spaces we did not create, so we make them more meaningful when we fill them with our possessions to make them uniquely our own.

When we feel ownership of a space, like where we live, it gives it a deeper meaning. We form emotional attachments with many spaces like our homes and communities. When we invest spaces with meaning it gives them value. The more people share meaning about a space and the more they are willing to do to get it, the more attractive it can become increasing its value including its monetary value.

We need a space to call our own. At home we might have our own room, desk, side of the bed, or our own chair in the dining room or at the kitchen table. We can even feel an attachment to space that is not ours. For instance, we might like to sit at the same table in a restaurant, the same seat on a bus or at the movies. If someone else is in our spot, it can make us feel uncomfortable. We feel this way because it reduces uncertainty giving us feelings of safety and predictability.

We can reduce uncertainty by having control over our own space. This is why when people experience difficulties they might clean the house, organize a desk, or rearrange the furniture. They may do this to assert control over something they can control to compensate for what they feel is out of their control.

• Ambience. The nature of our space can have an emotional impact on how we feel that can affect our behavior. When we see things in nature like mountains, a sunset, or a waterfall we may feel exhilarated or a sense of awe. This is because space can motivate an emotional response affecting how we feel. We can have similar emotional responses to the physical spaces we use everyday like our homes and workplaces. When we find them attractive it can give us a warm, positive feeling. When we find them stark or cold it can have a negative or depressing affect on how we feel.

Ambience affects the feelings and emotions we get from our physical environment. Candles or a fire in the fireplace can affect how we feel, helping us to relax or set a romantic mood. We use lighting, color, music, furniture, artwork, floor coverings, and wall coverings to create spaces that have a particular mood or feeling. Our possessions can also make us feel good. We decorate our spaces so we will feel safe, secure, and comfortable.

• Geographic affiliation. Another way we share meaning and reduce uncertainty about space is through geographic affiliation. Geographic affiliation refers to any place that we may feel a connection to like a neighborhood, community, city, state, region, or country. This could be where we were born, where we grew up, where we spend time, or where we live now. We may feel a connection with places we have only visited or have never seen in person like where our ancestors came from.

A geographic affiliation can become a part of our self-concept and how we see ourselves. We may feel a connection to places through our family history, heritage, culture, ethnicity, religion, or personal interests.

• Relationships. The way we use space can communicate the nature of a relationship. When we do not know someone very well we keep our distance. As we get to know someone, we are more comfortable being closer to them. The space between people can often indicate the type of relationship they have. Generally, the closer the distance, the closer the relationship.

These are types of physical space between ourselves and others.
• Public space consists of the spaces we occupy when we are out in public. We have little control over them, so they can have a higher degree of uncertainty.
• Social space involves every day interactions with others like going to the store or work. It allows us to directly communicate with others, but keeps them out of our personal space.
• Personal space is being close enough to have a private conversation or to touch the other person. We use this space in more personal relationships with friends and family. If someone we do not know very well enters this space we might feel uncomfortable.
• Intimate space is the closest we get to another person. We are close enough to communicate verbally and touch them physically, so we only allow a few people to get this close.

When it comes to space, we have conflicting needs and wants. We need to spend time with others, but we also need time to ourselves. When we say we need our space, what we mean is we need our own mental or emotional space, so that we can have some time to ourselves to think or relax.

We need a physical space to call our own and psychological space for our mental well-being. Others might think we should spend time with them, when we may just need time to ourselves to work things through. When we feel stressed, we may need time to process new information. It's helpful to be aware that when people say they need their space, it is for their own well-being and not necessarily a rejection.

We also need control over our space or turf, which are the areas where we feel we have knowledge, expertise, or responsibility. For example, at work we may write the reports or schedule the meetings. If someone else does it, we may feel they are invading our territory. This can create tension or conflict when others invade our space even if they are not aware of it.

Sharing space with other people can create tension, so they might stake out their space with their possessions. For example, siblings or roommates may leave clothing and other items lying around to claim their space. In relationships, we may leave items like a toothbrush or clothing at the other person's place. People use their possessions to let others know that this space belongs to them.

Other people's perception of your space can affect their perception of you.

The spaces we occupy at work communicate our status, importance, and position. Space is used as a reward for achievement. Executives occupy the largest offices in the most desirable locations to communicate importance and prestige. Space is used as an incentive for working hard and following the rules.

We like to personalize our workspaces by displaying artwork, books, plants, or photographs. Be aware that these things communicate information about you as well as letting others know that it is your space. We do this to make our space more familiar and comfortable, which can make work more enjoyable. We tend to work better and get more done when we are in a space that we find enjoyable.

Before putting out your personal items, look around to see how others personalize their spaces. You may want to emulate what other people do, at least until they get to know you. If other people perceive you as not fitting in they may be less likely to get to know you. If your space looks familiar it helps to reduce uncertainty, so they may be more likely to get to know you.

Time Management

Time is our most valuable resource because it is our most limited one. While we all have different amounts of resources available to us like money or space, we all have the same twenty-four hours each day. We can make more money, but we cannot make more time. So, managing time effectively is an important skill. How we spend time communicates a great deal about us, our interests, our priorities, our values, and who we are.

Since time is our most limited resource it creates value. We might judge the value of things by the time that we put in to them. We value relationships where we spend time and we spent time in relationships we value. We describe time in monetary terms like spending time, saving time, investing time, and time is money. Because our time is limited we cannot spend it on everything we want to, so we have to make choices and set priorities.

How we use time communicates what is important to us.

Social reality contains rules that tell us how to use time. Some cultures structure time, dividing it up into increments stressing punctuality and timeliness. Other cultures view time as flexible or relative. For example, if you were invited to a dinner party, in one culture you would be expected to arrive precisely at the time you are invited. In another culture, you might come fashionably late. In another culture you would come when you can.

• Punctuality. This is being on time and it is important because of what it communicates about us and what we think about others. Being punctual is a sign of respect and courtesy. Not being punctual can be perceived as being rude and inconsiderate of others. When someone is late, people may become offended because they think you are wasting their time, whether it's intentional or not.

• Timing. There are times when people are more receptive to your message and times when they are less receptive. By increasing your awareness you can use timing to tactfully communicate information. Timing can make the difference between being accepted or rejected, being perceived as respectful or rude. Timing can be based on the perception of urgency, necessity, and importance. It is important to choose an appropriate time and place to communicate, so you can achieve your desired outcome.

• Motivation. By paying attention to the timing of events and looking at what events preceded someone's actions, we can infer their motivation. If two events occur at the same time, we can look for connections to see if they are related, if one caused the other, or if it was just a coincidence. This is the difference between causation and correlation.

• Perception. Perception can be different than reality, so it can help to know how you are spending your time and what that communicates to others. We might think that we are spending a lot of time on something, but in reality we are spending very little time on it. For instance, we may feel that we may be spending lots of time with our family, but in reality we are not meeting their expectations.

We never have enough time to fulfill all our needs and wants, which means we have to make choices and set priorities. This creates tension between conflicting needs and wants, so you can end up spending all your time on short term needs, putting off long term wants.

This can leave you feeling frustrated or unhappy, and wondering why. By understanding how you spend your time and what that communicates to others, you can increase your awareness to give yourself more options to balance how you use time relieving tension and reducing frustration.

Do you feel that you have enough time to get everything done you need to do? Do you feel that your time could be better spent on things you want to do?

In order to more effectively utilize your time, from memory write down on a piece of paper everything you have done in the last month. Next to each item write down how much time you think you spent doing each one.

Now take your calendar and look to see how much time you actually spent doing these things. This will tell you how accurate your perception of how you use your time is, because perception can be different than reality.

On another piece of paper, write down each thing you want to do during the next month and how much time you want to spend on each. Then put that list away where you won't see it. For the next month, keep a detailed calendar of what you do and how much time you actually spend on each item.

At the end of the month, compare your calendar to the list you wrote at the beginning of the month to see how it compares. This will tell you how accurate your perceptions are so you can adjust your time to do what you want to do.

To better organize your time it can be helpful to consider the following.
1. What you need to do. These are things you must do in order to live.
2. What you have to do. These are everyday things you do, but could live without.
3. What you want to do. These are fun things to do that make you feel good.
4. What you ought to do. These are the things you know you should do, but don't.

Life would be much easier if we could do all of these things, but we have limited resources. Deciding what to do can be a source of conflict because doing one thing can keep us from doing others.

Imagine it's Sunday morning and you need to get groceries, have to clean the house, ought to go to church, and want to sleep in. You must be to work by noon, so you cannot do all of them. Which one do you choose?

By increasing your awareness, you can see how you are actually spending your time. By doing an audit and creating a budget of your time, you can organize your time based on both short and long term priorities to use it more effectively.

Writing it down on paper helps to clarify your perceptions, so you can have realistic expectations. Once you are aware of how you spend your time and how you want to use it, you can make changes to use it more effectively.

Money Management

There is an old saying that goes, money talks, so what does it say about you? After time, money is usually our second most limited resource. How we spend our money communicates our values, interests, and priorities. It communicates information about what our priorities are and what is important to us.

Money is a means by which you can get things done and make things happen. There are two ways to get something done; we can take the time to do it or we can spend money and have someone else do it. Most things that are created by people are a factor of time or money, or both. We spend our time to make money and we spend money to save time. This makes money a form of concentrated time.

We can improve how we utilize money by increasing our awareness and options. Keeping track of how we spend our money can increase our awareness of where it goes to use it better. We are more likely to save it when we know where it goes. Keeping a ledger of income and expenses like businesses do can help you to get a handle on exactly where every dollar goes.

Set aside a separate workspace like a desk and a filing cabinet to keep records organized. Use file folders for each month and one for unpaid bills to keep them organized. Conduct business only during the business hours you establish.

It can help to separate essential from nonessential spending. Essential spending pays for our needs like food, housing, utilities, and taxes. Nonessential spending is for things we want, but can live without. Start with essential spending and follow with nonessential spending to use your money more effectively.

There will always be good and bad years, so in good years it's important not to spend money just because you have it. Separate income from spending, so you don't spend everything you earn and can put money aside for when times are bad.

It's not what you make, it's what you spend. Cash flow is more important than income. If we spend all we take in we will never get ahead no matter how much money we make. This is how wealthy people can go bankrupt.

The secret to financial success is to live beneath your means.
By spending less than you make, you create a cash reserve.

That means making smarter choices to improve your cash flow by spending less than you make. To do this, determine how much you need to spend to be comfortable, rather than determining how much to spend based on how much you make. Otherwise you may be tempted to spend money just because you can.

When it comes to managing money, using a business approach can help. This involves making monthly income and expense statements, a year end summary, a budget for the next year, and future financial projections. You might have separate accounts to set aside money for important expenditures. For instance, set aside some money for fixed monthly costs to cover needs you can't live without like housing, taxes, and insurance.

Consider how these different types of spending can affect your economic stability.
*   Consumable. These are goods or services that are used up or discarded. They have little or no value soon after we purchase them. They include things that fulfill many of our most fundamental needs like food and energy.
*   Durable. These are things that lose value at a slower pace. They fulfill needs and wants for many years, but lose much of their value. These include vehicles like a car, clothing, and appliances.
*   Appreciable. These are things that can gain value over time. They can be a major investment like a house or smaller ones like antiques or collectibles.
*   Speculative. These are assets that can gain or lose value over time. They include stocks or commodities like gold.
*   Static. These assets are relatively stable over time. They may collect interest to keep pace with inflation. They include cash and savings accounts.

We have to spend money to fulfill our needs and wants, and what we spend it on can affect our economic well-being. While we should buy appreciable assets, most of what we buy are consumable items.

If we need money we may have to sell appreciable assets to buy consumables, reducing our economic security. So, it is important to purchase appreciable items, like a house. We all need shelter and buying a house turns rent, a consumable, into an appreciable asset. This helps to maintain financial stability by creating wealth, so we can keep more of the money we earn.

There are times we might spend more than we make, like when we get an education, buy a house, or start a business because we expect our income or the value of our investments will increase, so we will be better off in the future.

Build a financial firewall to reduce uncertainty and protect your future. A home is your best investment because we all need shelter and home ownership creates wealth.

Put some money aside as a cushion in case of unemployment in a low-risk government insured account. Also, have home, car, health, and liability insurance to protect yourself from unforeseen financial losses.

Creating a financial firewall and having a cash reserve increases your financial security because some kind of financial difficulties are sure to happen. Planning ahead and being prepared reduces uncertainty and helps insulate you from unexpected and undesired outcomes.

Chapter 10
Be Happier in Your Relationships

What if you had to move away from where you live now to a place where you didn't know anyone? What if you had to leave behind everyone you know including your family, friends, neighbors, and coworkers, and not have any contact with them? What would you do?

While we will probably not have to make all new relationships at the same time, thinking about this can help us to better understand how we have developed the ones we have now. This chapter is about how you communicate with others to create and maintain relationships.

Throughout our life we meet new people and develop new relationships, while others fade away. This is such a natural part of life we usually don't pay much attention to it because we are constantly going through the process of forming, maintaining, and ending relationships. So, what would you do if you had to form all new relationships?

We form relationships because they can be fun and enjoyable.

We use the word relationship to describe the connections we make with people like our friends, family, spouses, coworkers, and neighbors. However, we might talk about having a good relationship with a neighbor, coworker, or store clerk. When we do this, we are referring to the positive climate of the interaction rather than making an ongoing reciprocated connection. We communicate with other people all the time without creating an actual relationship.

For the purpose of this book, relationship refers to the connections we make to communicate with other people on an ongoing basis. In order to create a relationship both people must have a similar understanding of the nature of that relationship. This includes shared expectations of ongoing future contact. This can be as simple as seeing someone at work or as complex as a family member.

Think about the people you communicate with every day. Who are they? Where did you meet them? Perhaps you know them socially as friends, professionally as coworkers, or intimately as family members. Each of these is a different type of relationship that varies from impersonal to intimate.

We were created by nature with needs and wants we cannot fulfill ourselves, so we form relationships to help us fulfill them. Without relationships, every time we had a need or want to fulfill, we would have to start over from the beginning. We would have to look for a way to fulfill it and find someone to help us do it. This motivates us to communicate with others to create and maintain relationships.

When we first meet someone and begin to develop a relationship the rules have not yet been fully established. This can create a sense of uneasiness or awkwardness. In order to get things started, we rely on familiar patterns of communicating following the rules of social reality. As we get to know others, we negotiate our own rules to govern the relationship.

We form relationships because they can be fun and enjoyable. They can fulfill our need for affiliation and companionship because we like being around other people. Relationships help us to fulfill important needs like relaxation, escape, and pleasure. They help us to reduce tension and to share interests with others.

Even in work situations where the focus is on getting tasks done, having social time is important to having healthy working relationships. Regardless of the type of relationship, the need to get things done and the social needs of the individuals should be balanced for a healthy relationship.

Relational Development

Have you ever felt like you acted in one way when you were with one person and a different way when you were with someone else? We can change our behavior depending upon who we are with because of the effect that they have on us.

This happens because we have variable and non-variable characteristics. Non-variable characteristics include things we cannot change like gender, ethnicity, or age. These do not change when circumstances change and they are the things that people are most likely to notice about us.

Variable characteristics are those things that change depending upon our circumstances. They are things like how outgoing we are, our sense of humor, or what we like to talk about. Variable characteristics are important because they allow our behavior to change depending on the nature of the relationship. For instance, we act differently when we are out with friends, at work, or in church.

Some personal characteristics can become dominant or regressive depending upon who we are with, the nature of the relationship, and the situation. We may be outgoing and have a sense of humor when we are with our friends and act more subdued or serious with our coworkers at work.

For example, imagine two musicians playing on the same street corner. If each of them is playing their own song it would be difficult to hear either one of them and it would probably sound awful. If they play the same song together it would sound much better.

If they play together, neither one has complete control over what the people passing by hear. People hear a combination of the two that neither can create by themselves.

When people in relationships behave as individuals, like the musicians, it can become hard work that can increase uncertainty. When people are aware of how relationships work, they can work together to make the relationship less stressful, less work, and more beneficial to both.

Since every relationship is a separate entity created by the people involved, it can develop its own personality. This is why we may act one way in one relationship and in an entirely different way in another.

We may even act in ways we do not expect. Since a relationship is a combination of the people who created it, we might feel that we have little control over it and feel unhappy about the direction it is going.

Relationships help us fulfill our needs and wants. When we are born, our family provides for all our needs. As we get older, we develop other relationships to help us obtain what we need like a job, family, home, and even a positive self-concept.

**Without relationships, achieving some of our
desired outcomes would be more difficult, if not impossible.**

Why we form relationships.
- When we are young, we form relationships with people close to us like our parents and family to fulfill our needs and wants.
- As we get older, we become more independent and we form relationships with people by choice like friends and classmates.
- We form relationships in order to fulfill needs and wants, and to achieve desired outcomes we cannot achieve on our own.
- We form professional relationships to earn income to fulfill monetary needs.
- We form personal relationships to help fulfill our social needs like being part of a group.
- We form intimate relationships to help fulfill our needs for closeness and intimacy.

Relationships can help us to;
- Fulfill needs and wants we cannot fulfill ourselves.
- Gain feedback from other people.
- Share our thoughts and feelings.
- Gain insights into ourselves from others that we cannot gain by ourselves.
- Get advice from a different perspective that we cannot see ourselves.
- Have someone to hear our ideas and give us feedback.
- Bolster our self-concept.
- Provide support because life can be challenging, discouraging, and difficult.
- Make life easier and the workload lighter.
- Have nurturing and support.
- Have a positive self-concept and make us feel valued and worthwhile.
- Feel like we make a contribution and that what we do matters.

- Share interests and do things with people to make them more interesting.
- Feel appreciated and loved.
- Make our experiences more meaningful by sharing them with others.
- Make our ideas more interesting when others appreciate them.
- Gain power, status, and respect.
- Elevate a person's status so they are seen as being important.
- Provide people with resources to achieve their desired outcomes.

Relationships make life more meaningful because we share thoughts, ideas, feelings, emotions, and aspirations to gain a different perspective giving them more significance. Perhaps these are some of the reasons why nature created us with needs and wants we cannot fulfill ourselves, so that we are motivated to form relationships with others.

Relationships can help improve our self-concept, but they can also damage it. People may say or do things that hurt our self-concept. They may be concerned about losing their sense of who they are to another person or to the relationship. The other person has a say over what we do giving them some power or control over us. So, we may avoid relationships when we feel another person could have too much control over us.

Not everyone looks to form relationships with everyone they meet.
- They might avoid them out of a fear of what might potentially happen.
- They may feel that being in a relationship will make them more vulnerable.
- They might avoid relationships if they feel it could violate their privacy.
- They may avoid relationships because of a feeling that others might ambush them, lie to them, have a hidden agenda, or try to manipulate them.

When someone doesn't want a relationship, it could be seen as rejection when they may have issues they are working through. Instead of saying so, they just avoid having a relationship. It is helpful to be aware that when we try to form relationships and they don't seem interested, we don't think it is a rejection of us.

Forming Relationships

Think about the people you know. How did you get to know them? Do you remember the first time you met? While we could potentially meet anyone to develop a relationship, we only make a connection with a limited number of people and most of them never develop into relationships because we have a limited amount of time and energy to invest in them.

We can not form a relationship with someone without first making a connection. The most common ways we meet people are those who we see through everyday activities like work, school, church, in our community, or doing errands. The closer their proximity, the greater the frequency, and the more intense the connection, the greater the likelihood of developing a relationship.

These are some ways we meet people to form relationships.

• Family. Members of our family are the first people with whom we develop relationships. These relationships are often the strongest and last the longest. Family relationships are structured and have specific labels that have societal and legal expectations like a parent, child, or spouse. However, each family can develop their own ways of expressing these relationships.

• Proximity. This is probably the single most important way we form relationships. These are people who are close to us like our family, friends, neighbors, or co-workers. In order to have a relationship with someone, we first have to meet them. We cannot have relationships with people we've never met. Typically, we meet someone face to face, but we can also develop relationships in other ways like by mail, telephone, or over the internet.

• Frequency. We not only have to make a connection with someone, we have to keep in contact with them. Frequency is how often we see someone over time. We can develop relationships with people who are not in close proximity, but with whom we have frequent contact. The more we communicate with someone, the higher the likelihood we self-disclose information about ourselves increasing the potential of creating a relationship.

• Intensity. This is the degree of contact we have with someone. If we see them frequently or spend a large amount of time with them, the intensity of the contact can help to create a relationship. Our most intense relationships are often with the people we see where we live and work. We can also meet someone and spent a lot of time with them, however, a short intense relationship tends to not last very long because when the intensity subsides, the relationship is not as sustainable.

For example, when we attend camp or a seminar we can develop close relationships and promise to keep in touch. However, this usually doesn't last very long. When people go back to their normal lives the intensity goes away and the relationship is unlikely to continue unless there is another connection to sustain it.

• Similarity. People create and maintain relationships with others who are similar to them because uncertainty is reduced. Since we like ourselves, if we perceive someone is similar to us we should like them. Similarity can include many qualities including similar likes, dislikes, interests, education, or work.

We are more likely to create relationships with people who have similar backgrounds like the same culture, education, ethnicity, or geographic affiliation. They may have similar tastes in food, clothing, or music.

They may have similar experiences, occupation, or participate in the same activities that we do. The more we find someone is similar to ourselves, the more we have to talk about to create interest in a relationship.

• Profession. After our family, our closest relationships are often developed through our work. This is because we spend the most time there away from home. We create relationships at work to get along with our coworkers to help us do our job better. It is easy to create relationships with them because we are in close proximity, spent a lot of time together, and often have much in common like similar knowledge and experiences.

We develop professional relationships to make work easier, advance our career, and earn more money. However, just like relationships created by short periods of intensity, if we leave our job, our work relationships are likely to fade away unless there is another connection to sustain them.

• Relationships in common. We meet others through people we already know like their friends, family, coworkers, and acquaintances. These relationships reduce uncertainty because we have something in common. It would seem these relationships should have a degree of transitivity. For instance, if we are friends with person A, and they are friends with person B, then we should be friends with person B. Since relationships are created between the people involved, this does not necessarily hold true. Just because one person we like is friends another, it does not necessarily mean we will like them or they will like us.

• Common ground. When we meet someone for the first time we tend to look for things we have in common to feel more at ease around them. Finding common ground gives us familiar topics of conversation to make connections with others to share meaning, which reduces uncertainty. This increases the likelihood of developing a relationship. We are more likely to develop relationships with people we find interesting and can engage in conversation. We are less likely to develop relationships with people that are difficult to talk to or who don't seem interesting.

• Attraction. We like to be around people we find attractive and who find us attractive. We find others attractive for many reasons other than just physical appearance. Attraction can be intellectual, emotional, professional, or psychological.

We are attracted to others because we find them exciting, interesting, considerate, supportive, or stable. We are attracted to people who like us, who make us feel important, who bolster our self-concept, and make us feel attractive. Attraction is a powerful motivating force because it represents our expectations of fulfilling future needs and wants. The perception of attractiveness can determine whether or not we pursue a relationship.

• Likeability. We like people who like us because they have good taste. They make us feel good about ourselves and bolster our self-concept. When others like us we feel accepted and valued. Being well liked is a powerful social reward because it helps reduce uncertainty and makes us feel more at ease. If someone doesn't like us it can increase tension pushing us away from them because no one likes to be around others who don't like them.

• Random chance. Sometimes we meet someone by chance and hit it off, becoming friends or perhaps more. When we meet them we may feel a connection, a gut feeling, or intuition that peaks our interest motivating us to pursue a relationship. These types of relationships can surprise us because they tend to go against typical methods of forming relationships due to their high degree of uncertainty.

Meeting People

When you introduce yourself to someone you have never met before, what do you say? What information do you include and what do you leave out? What do you say first, second, or last? Do you talk about your work, family, past experiences, or interests? Do you introduce yourself the same way in every situation?

How we choose to introduce ourselves is influenced by the rules of social reality, our perceptions and expectations of the situation, and the people we meet. How we do this is the process of identity management.

Next time you meet someone for the first time, think about what you say about yourself. If you have time, afterwards write down what you and the other person said. Writing it down helps you to think about what happened. Doing this can help provide insight into how you perceive yourself and your expectations about how you would like others to perceive you.

Creating a good first impression comes from being confident, self assured, and friendly. If we are at ease, it makes other people more likely to be at ease with us. If we are uptight, nervous, or forced, they are less likely to feel comfortable.

When you meet someone, what do you communicate?
Verbally? Nonverbally?

Identity management.

Identity management is how we determine what to say and how to behave when we communicate with others. It would be inappropriate to communicate everything about ourselves because that would be overwhelming. So, we make choices about what information we communicate about ourselves to others. Identity management is how we communicate with others to shape their impressions of us.

These are some options people use to manage their identity around others.

• Agreeable. We want to be liked by others because it makes us feel good about ourselves. No one wants to be around someone who is disagreeable, difficult to get along with, or unpleasant. We like people who are agreeable, but it is a matter of balance because being too agreeable can be perceived as being phony or weak. People who are confident in themselves are more able to agree and disagree while expressing their own thoughts in an honest and friendly way.

• Helpful. We want to be perceived as someone who is helpful and supportive because no one wants to be in a relationship with someone who is not. We want to be helpful because it is the right thing to do and we want others to be helpful and supportive in return. Being helpful is good to a degree, however, people who are overly helpful can be perceived as clingy or trying to manipulate others for their own gain.

• Empathetic. We like to be around others who listen and empathize with us by seeing things from our perspective. We like to be around people who are open to our ideas and point of view. We like being around people who are sympathetic, nurturing, and compassionate because it fulfills an important need for support and security.

• Humor. Humor works to reduce tension and makes people feel at ease. We like people who have a good sense of humor because being too serious is no fun. However, someone who makes jokes or does not seem to take things seriously can be annoying. Everyone has a different sense of humor, so what one person finds funny another may find offensive. Hold off on using too much humor until you get to know someone in a more serious manner first.

• Etiquette. Etiquette and manners are the behavioral expression of the rules of social reality. Manners govern our behavior and how we communicate with others. We use them to manage our identity and make a positive impression on others. We use them because this reduces uncertainty, so others will perceive us as stable and trustworthy, helping them to be comfortable with us.

• Success. We want to be perceived by others as being successful. We can do this in many ways like having a good job, income, relationships, family, or being good at what we do. We communicate success by talking about our accomplishments, our family, and things that we have done. We do this because we want the respect of others, however, overdoing it can give others the perception that we are only trying to impress them.

Conversation

When we want to meet someone we need to make a connection with them. A good way to make a connection is through someone you both know. If you can have them introduce you, it reduces uncertainty making you less threatening. If this is not feasible, you might find a reason to talk to them.

One of the most common ways to meet someone is by engaging in conversation. In practically all aspects of life, conversation is an important skill because it is how we meet and get to know others on a more meaningful level. We have many conversations every day with our friends, family, and coworkers. We usually don't think much about them because we do this all the time. However, conversation is like other skills, that can be developed and improved.

There are times when having a conversation with someone is natural and easy. At other times it may seem difficult and next to impossible. No matter how comfortable or uncomfortable we feel conversing with others, communicating skills can be developed and improved.

Whenever we meet someone we don't know, there is a natural uneasiness, awkwardness, or tension. This feeling comes from the high degree of uncertainty we feel when we don't know much about someone. Developing conversational skills can help ease the tension and reduce uncertainty to create a more pleasurable experience.

We engage in conversation to develop personal connections that enable better working relationships. Most people do not talk only about their work, they also talk about their family, friends, experiences, likes, and dislikes. People want to work with others who not only can do their job, but who are enjoyable to work with as well.

In order to reduce apprehension and develop conversational skills, it can be helpful to practice talking to people you come in contact with while doing everyday tasks. You can talk about something that is familiar to you or that you enjoy.

When you first talk to someone there is always the chance that they will not respond. This can put you in an awkward situation. Should you say the same thing again or try something else? Instead of opening with a line, get the conversation going by asking open ended questions. Then, if there's no response it's okay to ask them again or ask another question.

- A question should be general in nature and not too personal.
- It should encourage the other person to reply with more than single word answers like yes or no.
- It should encourage the other person to talk about themselves.
- Asking them what they think or how they feel about something shows that you are interested in them.

Anticipate potential questions the other person might ask you and have short, to the point answers ready. If you have to think about it for too long they may think you are not being honest or making it up.

The situation or circumstances can help give you an opening question like asking for directions or if the other person knows someone you know. This gets the conversation going because they are not overly personal and they can easily answer them by saying more than just yes or no.

Have a couple questions in mind to initiate a conversation that can fit various situations. Don't over rehearse what you are going to say or use clever one liners because they could sound phony or insincere.

Start with familiar topics of conversation.

- Have a few topics in mind so you don't stand there staring at them trying to think of what to say next because the conversation will end if you don't have anything to talk about.
- Talk about subjects that you know something about and look for ones that you both are interested in to keep the conversation going.
- Avoid topics that are overly personal, complicated, controversial, or ones the other person may know little about.
- Let the situation work for you by talking about something close at hand like why you are there or what's going on around you.

At an appropriate moment in the conversation you might introduce yourself. You might tell them your name, what you do for a living, where you are from, or your interests. Ask the other person their name and repeat it once out loud. Saying their name communicates that they matter and helps you to remember it.

All too often we hear a person's name once when we first meet them and then forget it. We might get to know them, but then can't remember their name and by then it's too embarrassing to ask them.

A good conversation is balanced, it has give and take.

- It is not a monologue or a soliloquy.
- Do not dominate the conversation, let the other person speak.
- Give the other person time to respond.
- If you are doing most of the talking, ask the other person what they think about something to restore the balance.
- The more the other person talks the less work you have to do.
- Be positive, do not be negative when you first meet someone or you will come across as a downer.
- Avoid saying whatever comes to mind, think things through before you say them.
- Start with basic information about yourself, and proceed in small increments based on what the other person says.
- Avoid information about yourself that's too personal or intimate.
- Keep the conversation light by staying away from controversial topics.
- People like to talk about themselves, but do not let that person be you.

Listen when others are talking.

- Actually listening to them should let you know what to say next by following up what they said.
- If you ask them questions and don't contribute information yourself you could come across overly intrusive.
- By listening and responding to what they say, a conversation develops and begins to flow naturally.
- If it doesn't, be ready with something to say.

Use positive nonverbal body language.
- Smile, nod your head, and gesture occasionally to indicate that you are interested in what they have to say.
- Make appropriate eye contact using moderation depending on your circumstances.
- Not looking at them can make you seem uninterested or rude and staring can make people uncomfortable.
- Eye contact indicates that you are interested in them and are listening to what they have to say.

Not everyone will engage in conversation for many reasons.
- They may be uncomfortable talking to people.
- They may feel they are not good at it.
- They may have had a bad experience in the past.
- They may be closed off, unreceptive, angry, or rude.

When people won't talk to us we might feel that there is something wrong with us and take it as rejection. However, there may be nothing you can do to change that because it is just the way they are.

No conversation lasts forever. It's better to wrap it up when things are going well instead of standing there after the conversation has withered and died.

Have some ways to gracefully wrap up a conversation. You might tell them you need to go, need to circulate, or need to see someone else. How you do it depends on the circumstances.

- Have a clear end to the conversation.
- Since it is the last thing you say they are more likely to remember it than your opening because now they know you.
- Clearly signal the end of the conversation, but not necessarily the end of the relationship. How this is done depends upon your desired outcome and what type of relationship you want to pursue.

A common ending is to say something like, "I have to go, but it would be nice to talk with you again." This leaves the door open for you to make contact with them again. It also gives them an opening to follow up if they are interested. It shows that you value them and are looking to continue the conversation sometime in the future. However, don't say this unless you actually intend to do it.

Self-Disclosure

Self-disclosure is how we share or disclose information about ourselves to others. It is how we share meaning to develop relationships because it is a more personal form of communicating than conversation.

Self-disclosure helps us to build relationships. We use it to help us fulfill needs and wants like income, career, safety, security, respect, self-esteem, affection, and intimacy. Self-disclosure has risks, but it also has benefits. It helps us to understand ourselves and others by reducing uncertainty and invest in others, so that we can create and maintain relationships.

Self-disclosure usually begins by sharing basic kinds of information and depending upon the nature of the relationship, then it may progress to consecutively more personal levels. The following are varying degrees of self-disclosure.

1. Impersonal. Impersonal self-disclosure is what we do in daily conversation. It involves small talk about topics that are of little significance like the weather, sports, current events, or our present situation. We have no problem sharing this information about ourselves with others. This level of disclosure involves very little risk and we utilize established patterns of communicating following the rules of social reality. If things go well, we may share more personal information.

2. Casual. As we get to know someone uncertainty is reduced, so we are more comfortable with them. We might talk about what we did that day, what we do for a living, hobbies, interests, likes, and dislikes. We might use this information to introduce ourselves to others that we share a connection, like our coworkers. This level of self-disclosure lets us get to know others with little risk. Our conversation is more personalized, but is still cordial and polite following the rules of social reality.

3. Personal. This level of self-disclosure usually occurs in relationships with closer friends and family. We talk about our past experiences, preferences, thoughts, and feelings. We begin to develop our own rules to personalize the relationship. This helps develop a feeling of closeness strengthening their commitment to the relationship.

4. Intimate. This is the highest level of self-disclosure with our closest friends, family members, and intimate partners like our spouse. The other person knows most everything there is to know about us. These relationships have the highest degree of commitment and often have their own rules. This level of disclosure has the potential for the greatest rewards, but also entails the most risk, which is why they can also have a high degree of tension or conflict.

It can be helpful to use these self-disclosure skills.

• Appropriateness. Personal information should be shared in an appropriate manner based upon the situation, the other person, and the nature of the relationship. You may have met someone for the first time who told you their entire life story. This likely made you feel uncomfortable because it's an inappropriate self-disclosure with too much information communicated too fast. Start with basic, publicly known information and gradually move to more personal information.

• Information. Use good judgment because some information is appropriate to disclose. Some things are better off not disclosed to anyone. In a new relationship we usually start with things that are commonly known about us. Once we get to know someone, we might share more personal information. Not everything is self-disclosure. Talking about the weather, traffic, or current events is not self-disclosure. Instead, it may be perceived as way to avoid having a real conversation.

• Others. We do not self disclose everything about ourselves to everyone we know. We make choices based upon the other person, the nature of the relationship, and how much the other person reciprocates. What we disclose is determined by how comfortable we are with someone. It can also depend on our past experiences. If we had a relationship that went badly, we may be reluctant to disclose.

• Location. Where we disclose depends upon what we share. General types of information can be shared just about any place when it comes up in conversation. Personal information should be shared in private so no one can overhear it. Many activities can be conducive to self-disclosure like going for a walk, having a cup of coffee, or making a meal together. Any activity that can be done together which takes little effort or concentration will allow you to focus on the other person.

• Timing. When we disclose information can make a difference in how it's received. The information should be relevant to what is happening at the time or reasonably soon afterwards. If we wait too long it can be perceived as if we were reluctant to share information or we needed more time to think of a better story.

When relationships advance to the next level it is often an appropriate time to share relevant information. It can be difficult to find a good time to share information. Disclose when the other person is ready to listen. Set aside a time for self-disclosure when both people can give it their full attention.

• Reciprocity. Self-disclosure works when one person shares information about themselves and then the other person shares similar information. Just because one person discloses information about themselves does not mean the other person will share the same information.

If one person thinks that they are disclosing more information than the other, they may feel they are doing more to contribute to the relationship. There may be reasons the other person is not disclosing. They may be simply unaware of the imbalance. They may feel uncomfortable sharing certain types of information. They may feel that some information is nobody's business but their own.

• Pacing. This is how much information we communicate over a period of time. It depends on how comfortable a person is with disclosure. Start with a go slow approach because you can always add additional information, you can't erase information you have already disclosed. More information is not always better. Sharing your life story or pouring your heart out does not necessarily increase trust.

Self-disclosure has risks, but it also has benefits.
Self-disclosure helps us to create and maintain relationships.

• Detail. This involves how much information we share with others. There are two dimensions to information, depth and breadth. Depth is how much detail or how much information we share about a specific topic. Breadth is the extent or variety of topics or information we share. In casual relationships, we may have moderate breadth, but little depth by talking about a number of topics with few details.

In business relationships we may have less breadth and more depth knowing more details about someone, but only about work related areas. In close personal relationships there is likely to be both depth and breadth of information because we know more details and more things about them.

• Awareness and options. Awareness is important to self-disclosure so we know how we are coming across to others. We can do this by observing their body language and nonverbal expressions to see if they look interested or uncomfortable. Awareness of a person's response is important to gage the appropriateness of the information you share. You always have the option of what information to share, when to share it, and with whom. Or whether to share it at all.

• Responding. Self-disclosure can be uncomfortable, so it's helpful to show that you support others when they self disclose. Use effective listening skills, provide feedback, respond appropriately, use positive gestures like eye contact and nodding your head, occasionally restate what they said, and ask questions to show that you understand what they are saying.

You can reassure them that you appreciate their sharing this information by paying attention to what they have to say. Consider their desired outcome. Do they want help, advice, or somebody to listen and support them? Telling someone they need to self-disclose more or they don't self-disclose enough is not a good way to get them to do it or to build a relationship.

• Nondisclosure. While it's important to communicate openly and honestly, the reality is there are times when nondisclosure is better. These are things where the risk of damaging a relationship outweighs any benefits of disclosure.

This could include information that is no longer relevant, potentially damaging, or hurtful to others. It may be information others would see as a violation of their privacy and their trust in you. Or it may serve no useful purpose in the current relationship.

For example, we might wonder if we should be in a relationship or should end it. If these thoughts go away, the consequences of disclosing them may not. The process of self-disclosure affects our self-concept, so what we disclose to others can have long term consequences.

Tension in Relationships

We enjoy being around other people, however, there can be times when we feel like we are working harder in a relationship than we should. There can be times when things don't feel quite right and we're not sure why. By understanding how we create and maintain relationships, we can have options to improve them, so we can feel better about them.

Tension is a natural and unavoidable part of life. It can be created by conflicting needs, wants, and desired outcomes. Relationships have their own needs and wants, and some of them may be opposed to one another creating tension. It can be helpful to find a balance between these needs and wants or it could create dissatisfaction that can undermine the relationship.

These are some conflicting needs and wants that can be a source of tension.

• We need to be with others as well as to be by ourselves. We form relationships because we need safety, security, closeness, and affection. However, we also need some space and time for ourselves. Since we cannot do both at the same time, these opposing needs are a potential source of tension. We may want to spend time by ourselves when our family or friends want us to spend time with them. By understanding these conflicting needs, a balance can be established between them.

• We need self-disclosure as well as privacy. We share information about ourselves to reduce uncertainty, create trust, and develop relationships. We want to know more about other people and they want to know about us. However, we also need privacy and our own space.

• We need to do things with others as well as by ourselves. We make decisions with others, but we want to make our own choices. We want help from others to get thing done, but we want to do some things by ourselves. By understanding this we can find a balance between being with other people and being on our own.

• We need stability as well as excitement. Relationships mean making a commitment, however, we also need excitement, adventure, change, and to do new things. Too much stability can create dissatisfaction or unnecessary unhappiness. Too much excitement can make things chaotic and uncertain. By being aware of this, we can find a balance to have stability while making things fun and exciting.

Giving Advice in Relationships

A benefit of being in a relationship is being able to ask another person for advice. Giving and asking for advice is one way we show others we value and support them. When people ask for advice, it is likely that they just want you to listen. They don't usually say, "I want you to listen," they say, "We need to talk." Then, they want you to tell them that they are right.

What they are looking for is your support by agreeing with them. Giving advice can be risky because if they take your advice and things don't work out, they might blame you. If they don't take your advice and things don't work out, they may also blame you for not being clear enough. If they do take your advice and it works out, they will be happy that they fixed their problem themselves.

Options for giving advice.

• Determine the other person's desired outcome. Do they want you to tell them what they should do or that they are right? Don't try the fix something before you know what they want you to because it could make them upset.

Most of the time people just want someone to listen and give them support.

• Determine your desired outcome. Why do you want to give the other person advice? This is determined by the nature of the relationship. We might give advice to help someone, to support a relationship, or so they will support us in the future. Sometimes we just want to feel needed or appreciated.

• Give them feedback. Instead of expressing your opinion, encourage them to talk by asking open ended questions that need more than a one or two word answer. Stay on track and stick to the point because it's easy to get sidetracked. Sometimes just talking about a problem out loud helps people see their situation in a new way.

• Acknowledge feedback. When giving advice be aware of the feedback the other person is giving you. Do they understand what you are saying and are they receptive to it? When you know what they want it's easier to get to the point.

• Don't make it a competition. A common response is to relate your own personal experiences to show that you understand what they are going through. However, this can become a competition to see who has had it worse. This changes the focus away from them to you. When someone asks for help or advice keep in mind that it is about them, not you.

• Have a reason or criteria. In giving advice it's helpful to have objective criteria or logical reasons for it. Doing this can make the situation less personal and lower the emotional intensity. This is helpful if we have to tell someone they are wrong or they should do something because it's based upon objective criteria not personal opinion, so it does not become a personal issue.

• Avoid clichés or popular advice. These offer little substantive information, so they are not very helpful. They can be overly general by not taking into account the individual characteristics of the person or the situation.

• Utilize effective communicating skills. Clarify what the other person is saying to make sure you accurately understand it. Restate what the other person says so they hear it coming from someone else. It can help to hear it from another person's perspective. They might decide it's not such a big deal after all.

• Awareness and options. Help the other person to see themselves as others see them. This can increase their awareness of themselves and the situation. Encourage them to consider other alternatives. Considering options helps them to look at what they know in a new light in order to reach a solution.

• Be honest. If you care about someone be truthful, but also be tactful even when it's difficult. There are times when people want to be told they are right, however, they also need to know when they are wrong. If you want to help them you should be straightforward and tactfully tell them that you think they are wrong and why.

No one wants to be told that they are wrong, so it's helpful to have a reason or criteria for your position. Telling them they are right would be easier, but they may eventually realize that they are wrong and wonder why you didn't tell them the truth.

• Support is not the same as approval. We may be reluctant to support someone or help them because we do not agree with them. Nobody wants to be told they are wrong, however, they may need support. It is possible to support someone and help them find a solution without approving of what they are saying or doing. For example, if someone quits their job and you disagree with what they did, you can still support them to find a new job.

In giving advice, consider that you might be wrong. Whenever we give support and advice we always think that what we do is best and that we have the right solution. Keep in mind that there's a chance you could be wrong.

Criticism.

Eventually we will find ourselves in the uncomfortable position of having to tell someone we disagree with them or that they are wrong. This can be difficult especially if we value our relationship with them.

A good approach is to ask the other person what they think. Consider what they have to say and after thinking it over, tell them your thoughts about it. Perhaps after they have had time to vent their emotions and consider the situation, they may see it from a different perspective.

• You might ask them if they have considered other alternatives.
• Avoid broad statements and generalizations.
• Avoid characterizing things in judgmental terms like good or bad.
• Focus on the specific issues rather than the individual person.
• Provide straightforward and honest feedback.
• Be considerate and tactful to maintain a positive relationship.

In giving critical feedback, consider the following approaches.

* Begin with something positive and try to make the information as positive as possible.
* Be truthful and straightforward, but tactful and considerate.
* Get to the point, avoid dragging things out any longer than necessary.
* Show support by emphasizing positive aspects of your relationship.
* Tell them that your purpose is to help them if they want help. If they do not, don't force things and consider other options.
* Avoid evaluative words like good or bad because they are overly general and can make things worse.
* Avoid overstating things. Keep them in perspective. Rarely is something a total disaster.
* Be specific. Stick to the issues. Limit criticism to only what is necessary.
* Carefully consider what to say beforehand to avoid saying something you might regret later.
* Limit your criticism because too much can be overwhelming. You may be seen as just beating them up.
* Stick to the issues by being objective. Avoid making things overly personal.
* Have some criteria for your criticism that is objective and credible. Be sure to tell them what it is.
* Don't force your criticism on others. Just because you have an opinion does not mean others have to accept it.
* Consider that you might not always be right, all the time.
* Take responsibility for your own opinions, don't just assume others share them.
* Remember the importance of the relationship. Is it worth the controversy?
* Be aware of how the other person is responding to you and adapt your approach as necessary.
* Know when to quit. There is a point when enough is enough. People either get it or they don't, so don't belabor the point.
* End upbeat. Reaffirm the relationship. Tell them that you support them.

People talk about constructive criticism,
but do we ever find criticism constructive?

Nobody likes to be criticized. However, being in a relationship involves taking criticism. In this sense, criticism should be considered similar to a critique, which is a review or assessment of various qualities.

People have a natural tendency to defend themselves when they are criticized. However, it's better to avoid becoming defensive because the other person may feel that they are trying to be helpful and you might provoke a defensive response in them. If you respond defensively, then you have given them something else to criticize. Be aware of the difference between offering criticism as a critique instead of just being critical.

The following are options for responding to criticism.

• Listen to what they are actually saying. We can easily jump to conclusions or make assumptions about what we think someone is saying. Often criticism is not as serious as what we assume it to be. You can't respond to criticism unless you understand what the other person is actually saying.

• Ask for more information. Have them clarify what they mean. It can be helpful to understand the full scope of the criticism before responding. Often criticisms are broad generalizations based on a few bits of information with little detail.

• Don't guess about the specifics. Clarify language that is unclear because they may not really know what they are talking about. Sometimes people use criticism to pressure others to say something they don't want to say.

• Avoid responding unless necessary. Not all criticism warrants a response. Just because someone criticizes us we don't have to feel obligated to respond. We can just listen to criticism and tell the other person that we will think about it without making any promises or commitments.

In responding to criticism, it's easy to use broad generalizations like they don't know what they're talking about. This doesn't really address the issue and can escalate the situation. There may be some truth in what they say and considering that they may be at least partly right may be helpful.

• Ask for feedback. Ask them what they would do in your position. That doesn't mean you have to do what they say, but it helps you understand their point of view and what the real issues are. By asking for more information and feedback you take the emotional intensity out of the situation. When people give criticism they are likely to expect you to be defensive and when you aren't, they may not know what to do.

• Be open to new ideas. You don't have to agree with everything people say, but be open to the possibility you might be wrong. We often have the perception that agreeing with criticism is a weakness, however, we might benefit from the observations of others even if we do not agree with them.

After we've had time to think about it, some of it could be good advice. By looking at something familiar in a new way, we might come up with an even better idea.

Giving Bad News in Relationships

It's easy to tell others something that's fun or positive, but nobody wants to give bad news. The best approach is to be truthful, but tactful and supportive. Present information objectively and then let others make their own decision what to do about it.

Some common approaches can make a situation worse like ignoring it, having bad timing, changing the subject, using clichés, or not getting to the point. We might do this to be nice or protect other people's feelings, however, this might make the situation worse.

Be truthful, but tactful.

Options for giving bad news.

• Think about what you're going to say before you say it. Don't jump in before you think things through so you don't say something you wish you hadn't.

• Be truthful, but be tactful. Think of the most tactful approach and run it by someone else you trust or practice it out loud where no one can overhear you.

• Stick to the facts. Use descriptive statements and avoid judgmental words like good or bad because they can make people more upset.

• Get to the point. Long explanations or sugar coating things only makes people more upset or angry.

• Limit the scope of the conversation to what's essential. It's easy to get sidetracked and digress into other issues that are better left for another time and may only complicate things making them worse.

• Choose an appropriate time and place when you have their attention without distraction and other people will not overhear or interrupt what you have to say.

• Avoid saying that you know how they feel. Avoid things like, "I've been through this before." While this may be true, it's easy to turn it into a competition.

• Listen to their reply and find something that you can agree with to show support.

• Let the other person know that they are important to you. Assure them that you have their best interest at heart. This can help them be more receptive to what you have to say.

• Think about how you would like to be told the same news. Even though we know that bad news will eventually pass and things will get better, we may need to hear someone else say it.

• Tell them you care about them. They will appreciate hearing you say that they are important to you or that you love them. Let them know that you will be there for them and support them.

Chapter 11
Be Happier in Your Family

Family is something we all have in common. It is an important part of our life. We are born into a family, grow up in a family, and may form a family of our own.

It is through our family that we learn about ourselves, others, and the world around us. It is helpful to understand how families communicate because of the influence they have in our lives.

The world is a big place and families help to make it smaller.

Families give our lives structure, stability, and security to reduce uncertainty. Families are brought together by the same forces that create relationships including proximity, familiarity, frequency, and intensity.

Families form our closest, most personal relationships because we often live with our family members, know them very well, see them often, and care about them.

We are motivated to be a member of a family to fulfill many of our most important needs and wants. From the time we are born, families provide many of our needs and wants until we can take care of ourselves.

Families help us to reduce uncertainty. It is from our families that we learn about what it means to be a person and how to function in society. In families we share our ideas and experiences with others and they share theirs with us. Families share meaning through traditions and rituals that are a part of their customs and culture.

We share resources with family members by investing our time, energy, and other talents in our family. Families provide the stability and structure necessary for their members to invest in lifelong relationships.

In families it helps to have an awareness of each other's needs and wants, perceptions and expectations, and desired outcomes. Families work together to allocate resources like time, space, and money. Families develop ways to deal with solving problems, making decisions, resolving tension, and managing conflict.

Some characteristics of a family.

• Uncertainty. A family helps its members to reduce uncertainty about their family, other members, and the world around them.

• Shared meaning. A family shares meaning about their family and what it means to be a member of the family.

• Investing. A family provides a means for members to invest in the family and in each other as well as protecting that investment.

• Identity. A family has a collective identity. Members know that they belong to the family and each member considers themselves to be a part of the family. A family communicates what it means to be a member of the family including its history, traditions, and rituals. Families give us our name, which communicates information about us to others.

• Connections. A family has a network of connections between members, which they use to communicate with each other and does not exist between people outside the family. Members often have a higher degree of interaction that creates an ongoing relationship.

• Desired outcome. Family members generally work together to achieve mutual desired outcomes.

• Needs and wants. Family members work together to fulfill their own, and other family member's needs and wants, as well as those of the family. Families allocate resources and make decisions, which gives the people who do this power and influence over the others.

• Rules, norms, and roles. A family has rules, norms, and roles that govern member's behavior. Most often these are informal and communicated verbally. Families have a process to get things done, make decisions, and resolve conflicts.

• Structure. A family has many types of structures. These structures create a hierarchy of roles and responsibilities. They determine things like how members utilize their resources, organize their spaces, and allocate their time.

• Commitment. Families have a high degree of commitment that helps its members feel close, help each other, and sacrifice their own needs for those of the family and other members. Commitment comes from the high degree of self-disclosure between members that reduces uncertainty to create trust and stability.

Families also,
• Make sacrifices, work hard, and support one another without necessarily expecting anything in return.
• Work together for their mutual benefit.
• Spend time together.
• Share their thoughts and feelings.
• Help other members to solve their problems.
• Ask other family members for their advice to solve problems and help them to make decisions.
• Show nurturing and support creating closeness and commitment.
• Help us build a positive self-concept by feeling appreciated.

Marriage

Marriage is the most formalized relationship we enter into because it creates both a spiritual and legal connection between two people. Marriage is the means by which society recognizes two people coming together as a couple. It is an institution ordained by the church and sanctioned by the state.

**Marriage is the only relationship where we pledge publicly
before our friends and family to forsake all others until death do us part.**

Many communicating skills that can be helpful in a marriage are found in other parts of this book including conflict, decision making, problem solving, listening, giving advise and bad news, anger, and time, space, and money management.

We all have perceptions and expectations about how well our needs and wants are being met in a marriage. However, a couple may not feel they are being fulfilled. So, it can be helpful to increase your awareness by writing down your needs and wants in a marriage. Then rank them in order of importance.

Write down your expectations for yourself, your partner, and your marriage. Then write down your perceptions of how well your expectations, needs, and wants are being met.

We think that we may know how we feel, but writing it down and talking about it makes us think it through because we have to communicate how we feel.

If you asked someone if their expectations were being met they probably would just say, yes. Having a list gives you a starting point to determine what things are working well and which things could use improvement. Once you know what they are you can develop ways to improve them.

It can be helpful to a relationship for a couple to consider these questions.

- What are my needs and wants in a marriage?
- What are my partner's needs and wants in a marriage?
- What are my desired outcomes in a marriage?
- What are my partner's desired outcomes in a marriage?
- What are my perceptions about our relationship?
- What are my partner's perceptions about our relationship?
- What are my expectations about our relationship?
- What are my partner's expectations about our relationship?
- Are those expectations being met? How could they be better met?
- Is there a gap between our perceptions and expectations that cause tension?
- What are our rules, roles, rituals, traditions, and norms of behavior?
- How do we communicate, make decisions, solve problems, and allocate resources?

These questions will get you talking about important aspects of your relationship. We have perceptions and expectations about how well our needs and wants are being met. If they are not being met it can undermine our commitment to the relationship creating tension.

These questions are not meant to be a comprehensive list, but rather a place to begin a conversation that can continue over time. They can help to reduce uncertainty, so that each person has a better idea of what to expect. They can help to share meaning so a couple can understand one another better. This can help a couple to build common bonds, so that they can invest in their relationship.

Increasing your awareness can help improve your relationship because no two people perceive everything the same. This approach can help you to better understand how you perceive yourself, your partner, and your relationship.

Sex

When it comes to sex, there is a lot of information about methods and techniques, but it can be helpful to think about sex in a different way.

Think of sex as making a connection to communicate with another person. So, what message do you want to send? Want to receive?

Sex can be considered an intimate form of communicating because we make connections with another person using all of our five senses. We see them, hear them, touch them, taste by kissing, and smell them or their perfume or cologne.

When we communicate, we use the process of communicating to share our Great Idea with another person. With sex it's sharing affection, support, pleasure, and caring. It can be helpful to have an awareness of what you communicate with sex and how it's being perceived to know how well your message has been received. Making assumptions about sex is a good way to be disappointed or frustrated.

If you want the other person to do something, let them know. If you want to know if they like something, ask them. People may avoid doing this because they feel apprehensive or embarrassed talking about these things. However, it's better to talk about them beforehand, so they don't create misunderstandings later on.

When it comes to sex we have lots of perceptions and expectations, but may be reluctant to communicate them. We may do this out of fear of rejection or getting hurt. We may think that if our partner loved us they would know what we want. The reality is that if we love them and want them to know what we want, we should tell them.

It's helpful to truthfully, but tactfully communicate our perceptions and expectations so that the other person knows what we would like from them and what they can expect of us. When we know what's expected we don't have to guess and we have a better chance of satisfying them and feeling fulfilled. Effective communicating helps to fulfill our expectations because if they are not fulfilled, we may be disappointed or frustrated.

**Sex makes a connection using all of our senses.
Perhaps this is why it is considered so sensual.**

In a relationship, each person can have different desired outcomes creating tension, perhaps even conflict. If both people have reasonably compatible desired outcomes it helps create commitment in the relationship. But, if they are distinctly different it could create unnecessary unhappiness or drive them apart. In order to avoid this it's helpful to communicate your desired outcomes.

Children

One of the reasons for forming and maintaining relationships like marriage is to raise children. A child can be one of the biggest challenges for a couple because this can change their relationship. This happens because the focus is no longer on one another, but on the children. (Parents or couple also includes a married or unmarried couple, partners, single parents, biological and adoptive parents.)

Having children can change the nature of a couple's relationship even before a child is born. This increases uncertainty, so they reduce it by developing relationships with people who have the resources to fulfill their new needs and wants.

A couple will need support from family, friends, and medical professionals. They will get to know people who share the same experiences, so they can learn from them. This can help give their own experiences greater meaning.

With the addition of a child, how a couple communicates will change. Before children, a couple communicates directly with one another all the time. When they have a child, their focus is now on their child. This means that they will no longer be spending nearly as much time and energy on each other. Then they may wonder why they don't feel as close as they once did.

With each child, a family will need to adjust their roles, rules, and structure to accommodate their growing family. How they communicate as a couple will also change. So, it's helpful to be aware of these changes because parents can end up spending their time and energy on their children leaving little for themselves.

When a couple starts a family, they may assume they have compatible desired outcomes. However, they may be different creating tension or conflict. Just because two people have compatible desired outcomes to get married does not necessarily mean that they have the same expectations when it comes to having a family.

In order to avoid unnecessary tension or conflict, it's helpful for a couple to share their perceptions and expectations with each other. Having children can be stressful as well as rewarding for a couple. It can leave them feeling frustrated, but they may not know why. So, it can be helpful to understand each other's perceptions and expectations to reduce tension that can cause frustration or unnecessary unhappiness.

In raising children we often rely on our experiences when we were growing up. We may emulate our parents because it's familiar and we are comfortable with it, so it reduces uncertainty.

To help, parents can ask the following questions.
*   What are my perceptions and expectations for myself when having children?
*   What are my perceptions and expectations for my partner when having children?
*   What are my perceptions and expectations for my children?
*   What are my and my partner's desired outcomes for having children?

These questions are open ended to encourage a couple to come up with their own topics to discuss based upon what is important to them. Since everyone is different, each couple's concerns will be different.

Having children changes a couple's needs and wants from focusing on their own to those of their children. They may put their children's needs and wants before their own because they feel it's the right thing to do. However, this can leave them feeling tired, overwhelmed, or overworked. It can exhaust their resources to a point where they don't have the time or energy to spend on themselves.

They may have less time to fulfill their own needs, which can put stress and tension on their relationship. They may neglect their relationship until it starts to erode or even fall apart. Single parents may not have time to invest in a new relationship. It is understandable that parents want to put their children before themselves, however, they may do so to the detriment of developing their own relationships.

**Parents need to take care of their own relationship first
because it's what keeps the family together.**

It is important for couples to put their own relationship first to keep their family together. Through awareness a couple can maintain their relationship by fulfilling their own needs while still providing for their children. Knowing how children can change their needs and wants will help keep their relationship strong.

For instance, before taking off in an airplane, adults are instructed to place the oxygen mask on themselves first before assisting their children. If they try to put the child's mask on first and they are not able to breathe, they cannot help their child. By placing it on themselves first, they can breathe, so they can help their child.

Children learn how to communicate and behave in relationships when they become adults by emulating their parent's relationship. If their parents are stressed, frustrated, or angry they may have a diminished ability to help their own children. If their relationship is weak or stressed they may not be as effective in their relationship with their children. If the parent's relationship is secure, then there's a much better chance that the parent child relationship will feel secure as well.

The talk.

Parents should talk regularly with their children beginning at an early age because there may come a time when a child has problems and they will need to have a talk with them. It is easy to use the first style of communicating by only telling them what to do. Instead, try using the third style by engaging them in conversation to encourage them to talk to you using the techniques outlined earlier.

Instead of the big talk, have lots of small talks.

This can begin an ongoing process of communicating with your children, so they trust you and feel comfortable talking about these things when they are very young and they will feel comfortable talking to you when they get older.

Parents might avoid doing this because they feel awkward or uncomfortable talking about subjects like sex or drugs. But it's better that you talk with them and that they come to you for advice rather than going to someone you don't know. Children will seek out information where they feel comfortable getting it.

These are options for engaging children in conversation, so they are comfortable talking with you.

- Instead of the big talk, start with small talks.
- Follow their lead, when they want to know something they will ask, so be ready to talk to them.
- Be truthful, but tactful and don't get bogged down in extraneous details.
- Keep information on their level and age appropriate.
- Don't try to cover everything all in one talk, if they want to know more they will ask.
- Encourage them to talk by asking them open ended questions.

Regularly communicating with your children not only provides information, it also reduces uncertainty about you so they know that they can trust you and can come to you when they need help. And when you know your children, you don't have to worry about what they are doing, because you know what they are doing.

As children get older, how you communicate with them will change to adapt to changing circumstances. They will be increasingly influenced by others outside of the family. This can give outsiders influence that could affect their behavior.

When they go to school, they will have a whole new communicating network. So, it's helpful to prepare them for this change by involving them in activities with other adults and children, so they are more adaptable to new situations.

Adolescence is a time of transition from being dependent upon our family to doing things for ourselves. It is a time when children begin to communicate more with others outside their family. How well parents have prepared their children for this can affect their behavior.

If the rules or structures are too rigid, they may resist them to get them changed. If rules and structures are more flexible, they may not see the need to disobey because they can make their own rules within the structure of the family.

United front.

In order to fairly enforce the rules, a couple must have a united front to avoid any overlap of authority that could cause confusion or conflict with children. While a common approach is for couples to share things equally, it can be more effective for each of them to have their own areas where each one is the only decision maker. This makes it less likely for children to try a divide and conquer approach, where one parent says one thing and the other says something different.

We have a natural tendency to want to protect our children from things that hurt them. However, by overprotecting them they may become less prepared to deal with problems, particularly when they become an adult and are out on their own. Instead, parents can help prepare their children by increasing their awareness about the problems they will face as they get older.

If uncertainty is reduced too much and everything is taken care of for them, they may not do the things they need to do for themselves to develop their own independence. Children and adolescents can benefit from a degree of uncertainty where everything is not taken care of by their family, so that they can learn to become self-reliant. Parents want their children to be better off than they are, but reducing uncertainty too much can do more harm than good.

Family resources.

Families have many kinds of resources, so they have to make decisions about how resources are allocated and who gets them. These resources include money, possessions, space, and time. This gives the family members who make these decisions power and influence over the others. This power can be used as a form of control to get the other members to conform to the norms and rules of the family.

We are likely to invest more of our own resources in our family than any other relationship because we have expectations of getting the benefits that only families can provide to fulfill many of our most important needs and wants.

Families can provide social rewards in ways that other relationships cannot. They can provide verbal praise, reinforcement, acknowledgment, support, respect, status, and prestige. These social rewards can be a powerful force motivating people to make a commitment to their family.

Being valued and accepted by others makes us feel appreciated bolstering our self-concept. Families can fulfill our needs and wants for acceptance, affiliation, and support. Conversely, families can use these rewards as a punishment by withholding them to enforce the rules.

If we feel we are not receiving fair benefits, it can be a source of tension and conflict. This is one reason why family relationships can be the most rewarding, as well as the most infuriating.

Families shape our self-concept by providing us with feedback.

We utilize reflected feedback to see ourselves as they see us. When we receive positive feedback, it bolsters our self-concept and self-esteem. When we receive negative feedback, it can be especially harmful because it comes from people we are close to and whose opinion we care about.

We have expectations about our family and perceptions about how those expectations have been met. Tension and conflict can arise when our perceptions do not meet our expectations. In order to avoid this, it can be helpful for family members to communicate their perceptions of how those expectations are being met.

Family traditions.

An important part of maintaining a family is participating in family rituals and traditions. Rituals are repeating patterns of communicating and behaviors that can occur at specific times or during family gatherings. Traditions are ways of doing things that are often passed down over many generations.

Families have every day rituals like having dinner together and annual traditions like celebrating birthdays, anniversaries, or holidays. Rituals and traditions are based on a family's past experiences, culture, religion, and geographic affiliations.

Rituals and traditions help a family fulfill many needs and wants.
- They provide for identity needs by letting people know who they are and where they came from.
- They provide for affiliation needs as people feel closer to others who share the same traditions.
- They fulfill the need for structure by providing regular recurring activities that give us a sense of stability and predictability.
- They fulfill our need to develop our self-concept by connecting us to others who share these traditions with past generations.

Family rituals and traditions often have a deeper meaning that is shared by everyone who participates. They have a history that has been developed over long periods of time. Participating in these rituals helps to create connections between family members. So, we look forward to celebrating these traditions every year.

Family Structure

Family structure consists of a family's roles, rules, and boundaries. Structure helps to organize a family to let everyone know who is responsible for what. Structure involves how families communicate, use time and space, and create boundaries.

Family structure can help to determine;
- Who makes the rules, decisions, and allocates resources.
- Who talks to whom, about what, when, and under what circumstances.
- Who is responsible for doing what things like helping with household chores.
- How family members use their space to make a house a home.
- How family members use psychological space, including turf or territory.
- How family members use their time.
- How a family schedules daily activities like when to wake up, have meals, and go to bed.
- How a family schedules dates throughout the year like birthdays and holidays.
- What family members will be doing together in the future.

Family structure can vary from strict to flexible. A strict structure provides stability to keep things together reducing uncertainty. A flexible structure allows a family to adapt to changing circumstances. Too much flexibility can make things more chaotic and unpredictable increasing uncertainty, which can reduce stability.

Being overly strict can hinder individual creativity, reduce options, make decisions more difficult, and create tension. A balanced approach between being strict and flexible allows for families to have options that takes into consideration each member's individual nature while maintaining the family structure.

Family structure includes boundaries, which can be open or closed. Closed boundaries don't allow people to move across them very easily, but they provide stability. Open boundaries allow people to move in and out more easily, but they may increase uncertainty.

Boundaries define who is a family member and who is not. Boundaries give members a feeling of belonging and being sheltered from the outside world. Boundaries provide safety and security, and gives them a feeling of being connected to others who belong to the family.

Internal boundaries often exist within a family and can separate some family members from others. One of the most common internal boundaries is between adults and children. Boundaries can have an affect on how family members communicate, share ideas, and interact with one another. They can influence how members communicate with one another and what they communicate about.

Some matters are only talked about within the family and are not shared with outsiders. Some things, like making decisions, may only be discussed between adults, while some topics may not be talked about at all. Informational boundaries determine what information members keep to themselves or share with others.

Family rules.

Practically all aspects of our lives are governed by some set of rules including our family. Without rules life would be chaotic increasing uncertainty. Rules are necessary for a family to function properly. They are important for children because they provide the structure and boundaries necessary for their development.

Families have rules everyone is expected to follow. However, some rules are unspoken, so we may not know about them until we break them. The rules need to be clearly communicated to everyone, so they understand what is expected of them.

When children get older, parents can explain why the rules are important, so that they will better understand why rules are necessary. As they gain more responsibility, children can have a say in making the rules because by having a say in creating them, they are more likely to follow them.

Children might test the rules to see if they will be enforced. So, it's important to be consistent, to clearly communicate the rules and fairly enforce them. When they are enforced, it's important they understand what they did wrong, so they can correct their behavior in the future.

If they ask why they can't do something, instead of saying, "Because I said so," it's better to tell them why so that they understand why rules are important. This makes them more likely to follow the rules, so when they get older they can make their own rules because they understand why families have them.

Rules need to be stable, but they also need to be flexible so that they can be changed as needed. If the rules are too strict, family members could justify breaking or ignoring them. If they are too flexible they do not serve their intended purpose.

Families need balance and a way to change the rules as needed, so it does not undermine the family structure. When children get older, they can have a say in creating some of the rules to give them more responsibility.

Family roles.

Families have tasks that need to be accomplished, which means somebody has to do them and family members need to know who is responsible for what tasks.

Since everyone cannot do the same things at the same time, individual members will specialize by taking on different tasks creating their roles. Family members often have multiple roles like being a parent, child, sibling, and spouse.

Having stable roles reduces uncertainty because everyone knows what they are supposed to do.

- Some roles are based on age, gender, or marital status.
- Some roles are only done by adults.
- Some roles are based on relationships like parent, child, and sibling.
- Some roles like parent and child don't change, once a parent, always a parent.
- Some roles change depending upon a family's needs and wants, like who does the cooking or cleaning.
- Some roles are based on a family's background, ethnicity, culture, religion, and geographic affiliations.
- Some roles are fulfilled based upon each member's interests or ability.
- Some roles are fixed while others are determined through behavioral reinforcement.
- Some roles are based on doing tasks like making an income, shopping for food, and doing household chores.
- Some roles fulfill a family's need for fun, relaxation, excitement, or adventure by planning activities to help relieve tension that can build up in families.

Behavioral reinforcement.

When family members fulfill a role and receive positive feedback from the others, they are likely to continue in that role. If they receive a negative response, they are less likely to continue. This is why it's important to give family members positive feedback when they do something helpful for the family.

There are times when a family member may exhibit negative behavior just to get attention. If they do something positive and do not get the response they want, it can be discouraging reinforcing negative behavior. So, receiving clear and consistent feedback helps to develop positive behavior.

Family tension.

The feeling that a relationship is hard work may be an indicator of underlying problems stemming from struggles over control, power, or allocation of resources. Developing clear norms, roles, and rules can help to relieve tension to help a family become more effective.

Relationships can feel like hard work because they are often a source of tension.
- Tension can come from differing perceptions and expectations.
- Tension may come from unfulfilled or competing needs and wants.
- Tension may come from not getting fair rewards for fair contributions.

Families can be a source of tension due to conflicting or unfulfilled needs and wants. Tension can come from being close to other family members, not only emotionally, but also living in close proximity.

Having family members talk about how well their expectations are being fulfilled or how resources are allocated can help relieve tension.

It can be helpful to be aware of these sources of tension.
- Family members need to spend time together, but they also need their own space.
- Family members need to feel a part of the family, but also have their own individual identity.
- Family members compete for resources like having their own room, space, and possessions.

Family members may wait until there's a problem, emergency, or even a crisis before they talk with one another. They may begin by saying, "We need to talk." Everyone knows this means that there is a problem.

This can make communicating stressful. In order to avoid members feeling that talking with each other is a bad thing, families can have regular times where everyone gets together to talk while doing fun activities like having milk and cookies, making crafts, or sharing a meal.

Having all family members involved in making the decisions that affect them shows that they are valued. They are more likely to support a decision if they understand why it was made and are part of the decision making process. When they know the criteria and reasons for making a decision it can help to reduce tension and conflict.

Families and Food

It seems that everyone is busy these days, so it's easy for family members to get wrapped up in their own activities. They may see little of each other and don't communicate. They may feel tension or distant from one another and then wonder why they don't get along like they used to.

Families can create activities to bring everyone together that encourages them to communicate with one another. These activities can become part of their norms, so everyone is included. They can be part of their regular routine, so they don't take up much time. One of the most fun and effective is cooking together.

It has become all too easy to eat something out of the microwave by ourselves. So, it can be helpful for families to spend time together preparing meals because it helps to fulfill many of a family's needs in addition to making something good to eat.

Families and food naturally go together. Food is an important part of a family's traditions and rituals like celebrating holidays, birthdays, and anniversaries. Preparing meals is part of what it means to be a family because it creates connections that bring people closer together.

By cooking and baking from basic ingredients,
children can learn about how food is made and why it's important.

Everyone likes to eat, so cooking together can be a fun family activity. Then the family can sit down to share and enjoy what they made together.

Cooking together can help bring families together.
* It can encourage family members to talk to each other.
* It can help them to share meaning because food is often connected to our past experiences, traditions, culture, and heritage.
* It can encourage investing in one another because they are spending time together.
* It can help encourage conversation.
* It teaches children important life skills like how to take care of themselves and their family.
* It teaches children how to follow a plan, how to budget, and how to choose and buy ingredients.
* It teaches children about food and where it comes from.

Families can develop activities that bring everyone together. It can be a time for them to talk to one another and spend time together.

They could make their own greeting cards for birthdays, anniversaries, or holidays. Then they can enjoy and be proud of them for many years.

Another activity families can do together is to make a book of rules for the family. All families have rules and children may try to get around them. They may not be aware of the rules or don't understand them.

Making a family book of rules can help children to better understand the rules and have input into making them, which can encourage them to follow them.

Relationships can be difficult. We might feel that a relationship is not going right, or did not turn out like we had hoped. This can leave us feeling upset or frustrated and we may not know why.

By understanding how uncertainty affects us, we can better understand how relationships are created and maintained. We can develop skills to communicate effectively with others that can help improve our relationships.

Chapter 12
Be Smarter in Groups

What if you went on a job interview, but you didn't know what the job was for? What would you say? What if you got the job and it was a really good job, so you didn't want to lose it, but no one told you what you were supposed to do. What would you do?

After you were there for a while, you still don't know what job you are supposed to do. You don't ask anyone because you don't want to look like you don't know what you are doing and don't want to get fired. Now what would you do?

While this may sound unlikely, you may have experienced something like it without even knowing it. When you join a group or organization it's likely that no one told you the unwritten rules that govern people's behavior.

Following the rules and norms of behavior can be more important to your success and job satisfaction than doing what you were hired to do.

All groups and organizations have rules that govern how people communicate and behave, and you need to know what they are.

The other members may or may not tell you what these rules are, so you might break them and not even know it. Knowing how groups and organizations work can help you communicate more effectively increasing your chances of success.

Professional communicating is about how you communicate with others to create and maintain professional and other types of relationships in groups and organizations.

Groups and uncertainty.

You have probably been a member of a group where things went well and you felt good about the group. You have probably also belonged to a group where things did not go well, so it felt like a waste of time.

This may have left you wondering what makes some groups more effective than others. Knowing how groups work can affect how you feel about a group because having a good group takes effective communicating skills.

Groups are a natural part of life, so it is helpful to know how groups work because of the influence they have on our lives. Groups provide resources, affect our self-esteem, influence our perceptions and expectations, and help us to achieve our desired outcomes.

Much of our life is organized based upon groups like our family, work, school, church, and community. Group members can be expected to invest their own resources in the groups they belong to including their time, energy, expertise, experience, and even material resources. They do this with the expectation of receiving benefits in return for their contributions. These benefits help them to fulfill their needs and wants.

Being a member of a group is a kind of relationship, so it can include many of the same characteristics that comprise relationships including proximity, frequency, intensity, and similarity. Defining what constitutes a group is similar to defining what makes a group of people a family. Most of the time a group is defined by the perceptions of the people involved.

Knowing how groups work can affect how you feel about a group because having a good group takes effective communicating skills.

The following are some characteristics of a group.

• Reduce uncertainty. Groups help their members to reduce uncertainty about the group and the other members.

• Shared meaning. Groups share meaning about the group, its history, and what it means to be a member.

• Investing. Groups provide a means for members to invest in the group and in each other and they protect that investment.

• Identity. Groups have a sense of collective identity. Members know that they belong to the group and consider themselves to be a part of the group. Groups often have names, logos, or perhaps a mascot. Members have a clear idea of what it means to be a member of the group including its traditions and history.

• Connections. Groups have a network of connections between members they use to communicate with each other that does not exist between people outside the group. Members often have a higher degree of interaction that creates an ongoing relationship.

• Desired outcome. There is a mutual purpose or desired outcome that members work together to achieve. In order to do this they have tasks that members need to accomplish. Groups have a sense of collective outcome as they generally succeed or fail together.

• Needs and wants. People are motivated to join the group to have their needs and wants fulfilled. They work together to fulfill not only their own needs and wants, but also those of the group. Groups allocate resources and make decisions, which gives the people who are in charge influence over the others.

• Rules. Groups have rules that govern their behavior. These are often informal and communicated verbally. Larger more formal groups might write them down in a handbook. Groups develop a process to get things done, make decisions, and resolve conflicts. Members need to understand how this process works, so they can work together to achieve their desired outcomes.

• Structure. Groups have many types of structures that vary from formal to informal. They may have a hierarchy of how members communicate and who makes decisions. Groups determine how members spend their time in the group. They often control physical space, like offices, and determine how that space is utilized. Members create their own psychological space, like territory or turf, by determining who is responsible for what things.

Types of groups.

• Family. Our family is the first group we belong to, so it can form our perceptions and expectations of how groups work. Our family is where we learn how to make decisions, resolve conflicts, vie for resources, and negotiate need and want fulfillment. As we get older, we become members of other types of groups.

• Naturally occurring groups. People have a natural tendency to get together with others in groups to share mutual interests and activities. We create groups with people who live in our community, go to the same school, attend the same church, work at the same place, or share common interests. We do this to make what we do more fun and interesting. Some of these groups develop naturally or spontaneously because of a common connection or shared interest.

• Purposely created groups. Some groups are formed intentionally in order to achieve a specific purpose or desired outcome. These groups tend to be task orientated like a business. They can also be socially orientated when people come together to share a common interest or hobby. We purposely create groups in order to participate in activities and accomplish tasks with others in a way that fulfills our mutual needs and wants.

• Newly formed groups. All groups have the same thing in common, at one time they did not exist. Every group has to be created, so when a group first forms its founding members all join at the same time. This means that members are likely to be on an equal footing because there is no past history. These groups experience a period of adjustment based on the law of uncertainty.

This time can be characterized by feelings of awkwardness because everyone is uncertain about what to expect from one another and from the group. If they know little about one another they will need to reduce this uncertainty through the process of self-disclosure. Newly formed groups have to reduce uncertainty by determining how the group will function including their structure, roles, norms, and rules. Until this happens, they may have a difficult time working together.

• Existing groups. Most of the time we join an existing group. When we join an existing group the other members already know one another, so they have a past history. They have already reduced uncertainty, shared meaning, and have invested in the group. They may have already developed the group's structure, roles, norms, and rules. This puts the new member at a disadvantage because they know less about the group than the other members.

Even though the group is established, when a new member joins it can put the group through a period of adjustment because they need to reduce uncertainty about the new member. A new member must get to know the existing members and how things are done in the group.

• Task groups. Just as individuals have needs and wants, groups have their own needs and wants to fulfill. Regardless of the nature of the group or how it is created, groups have tasks that need to be accomplished in order to function.

The most common purpose for forming a group is to accomplish tasks, because more people working together can accomplish more tasks faster and more effectively than individuals can by themselves. Task groups can be formal in nature, like in a business, or they can be more social. Even social groups have tasks that need to be accomplished for the group to function effectively.

• Social groups. Some groups are formed to fulfill the social needs of its members. They are generally more informal and casual. All groups have social needs because working all the time is no fun and does not make a group very attractive or satisfying for its members. Even if the purpose of a group is to accomplish tasks, it may not feel very satisfying. This can happen when the social relationships are not well developed.

Members need to accomplish tasks, but they also need enjoyment, relaxation, and to just have fun. Every group has to find its own balance between fulfilling task and social needs to be effective, because they both cannot be fulfilled simultaneously. They might set aside time before and after meetings for members to socialize and talk informally with one another. The group can celebrate rituals and traditions. They can spend some time together in social activities when they are not working on a task.

• Teams as groups. Some groups are referred to as teams and their work called teamwork. A team is always a group, but a group is not necessarily a team. A team is usually a part of a larger organization. They may use sports metaphors to help make the group successful.

A team is often a specialized type of group formed with a clearly defined desired outcome. They are generally more focused and structured with a strong sense of commitment, loyalty, and group identity. Teams function much the same as groups, so when we talk about groups it also refers to teams.

How Groups Are Formed

How do we meet people to form groups? Sometimes it's by choice and other times it's by chance. Sometimes it's a bit of both. Groups are formed by communicating with others about common interests, but we first have to meet them by making a connection. Since we are only able to come in contact with a finite number of people, we have limited options of what groups we can join.

We often rely on familiar patterns of communicating that follow the rules of social reality. We form groups to help us fulfill needs and wants we cannot fulfill ourselves. The advantage of joining groups is that they can help us to fulfill some of our needs and wants on an ongoing basis rather than negotiating with someone every time we need something.

These are some of the ways we meet people to join a group.

• Family. Our family is the first group that we belong to, it's where we learn how to communicate and behave in groups. A family usually has a hierarchy of clearly defined relationships and roles like parent, child, and sibling.

A family is a very specialized type of group because it is more dependent upon the individual relationships between members to create the group rather than the group creating the individual relationships between its members.

Families are the most effective form of group
because they have the ability to fulfill our needs, wants, and
desired outcomes, which is why they are the foundation of society.

• Proximity. We form groups with people who are physically close to us, who share the same geographic or professional space like our neighbors or coworkers.

• Frequency. This is how often we communicate with other people over a period of time. The more often we communicate with others, the greater the likelihood of forming a group.

• Similarity. We form groups with people who have a similar background, experience, education, ethnicity, culture, or geographic affiliation. They may have similar tastes in food, clothing, sports, politics, or music. We do this because the more we find someone is similar to us, the more uncertainty is reduced and the more we have to talk about.

• Intensity. This is the amount of time and energy we spend with others. We share a higher degree of intensity with people like family members or coworkers. Intensity is likely to go away when we leave the group. This is why seminars and team building exercises work in the short term, but can lose their effectiveness over time.

• Profession. We join groups at work to get things done, to make work easier, and to further our career. We form task groups help get things done and social groups help make work enjoyable. Groups can be created for a specific purpose like a company department or team.

• Common interests. We form groups to share common interests, activities, sports, and hobbies. Forming groups helps us to share knowledge, experiences, and resources to enhance our own experiences and share things we enjoy with others. This helps group members benefit from the experience and knowledge of others.

• Connections in common. We join groups because we know the people who belong to them. We may decide to join a group they belong to so we can spend more time with them or with people who we perceive are similar to us. Groups often use members' connections to recruit new members to join them.

• Attractiveness. Groups are attractive because they convey status, prestige, and respect. These qualities can be transferred from the group to its members. We like being around people who are interesting, attractive, intelligent, thoughtful, helpful, or who like us. This can make us feel valued, bolstering our self-concept.

• Likeability. We like people who like us because it makes us feel good about ourselves and bolsters our self-confidence. Approval of others is a powerful motivating force because it is a significant social reward. When people don't like us it increases tension and pushes us away from the group because no one likes to be around others who don't like them.

• Random chance. Every once in awhile we find a group of people where we just hit it off. This is unexpected because they tend to not fit in with typical methods of forming groups due to their increased degree of uncertainty. We may find a group attractive because of a high degree of uncertainty, which gives it a feeling of mystery, excitement, or adventure. Or we may feel a connection or gut feeling that catches our interest motivating us to join.

Balancing the Group

A group is only as effective as the individuals that comprise it. Choosing group members may be the single most important task facing any group. This makes the process of selecting who is in a group important to its success. Some groups develop naturally and members have little or no choice over who is in the group.

Some groups are created to achieve specific desired outcomes, so there may be rules to determine who can join. Other groups have restrictions or requirements on who they allow in the group to maintain a perception of exclusivity or the professionalism of the group. They may have requirements like earning a degree or passing a test to maintain professional standards and public confidence in the group. Having some criteria for members helps the group to be more effective.

To create a group that works well together takes balance. Balancing a group involves balancing the roles people play within the group. It is finding the right combination of experience, skills, and expertise relevant to the task. It also takes the right combination of communicating skills. For example, a group made up of all leaders may have a more difficult time working together in a group than one that is more balanced with people who have experience in more supportive roles.

In choosing members for a group, consider what they bring to the group. While it is important to give consideration to their expertise and work skills, they also bring with them their communicating skills, behavior, attitudes, and past experiences. Consideration should be given to their social skills and ability to work with others. People may be good at what they do, but they might have difficulty working in a group with others.

Choosing effective group members is the most important task for any group.

Group size.

To balance a group, consider the best size to achieve the group's desired outcomes. A group needs to be big enough to accomplish its task, but not too big to detract from it. Size depends on the resources that will be needed, the task to be accomplished, and the individual member's abilities.

A workable size allows each member to communicate directly with every other member. Generally, it takes three or more people to be considered a group, but a more practical size can be from five to around twenty members. If a group is going to make decisions that involve voting, it must have an odd number of people to prevent tie votes.

There are advantages and disadvantages to both small and large groups, so it's helpful to be aware of them to choose the best size for your group. Larger groups have more resources, information, experience, and expertise, but this does not mean that they make better decisions than smaller groups. They can handle more work by breaking a task down into smaller tasks and assign them to individual members to get them done more efficiently.

However, large groups may need more structure to function. A few people may dominate the group while others may hold back and not contribute as much. They can fracture or breakup into smaller groups with cliques of members communicating amongst themselves.

Larger groups have fewer interactions between members and less time for each person to have their say. They can be difficult to control and take more time in making decisions, or may need to vote. Members of larger groups can be more likely to feel disconnected, be dissatisfied with the group's decisions, and have less satisfaction with the group.

Smaller groups tend to be more informal because everyone can meet face to face so they can communicate directly with one another. They are likely to make decisions faster, have less dissent, and are less likely to have tension or conflict. Everyone tends to participate because they aren't able to hide or go unnoticed.

Smaller groups are more likely to have fewer rules and make decisions based upon consensus. They are less likely to have hierarchies, so everyone is on the same level as everyone else. It can be easier to find a common time and suitable space where everyone can meet.

However, a smaller group has fewer members to bring in information and resources than larger groups. They may need to rely more on connections to other people or resources outside of the group to get things done. They may become overworked leaving them feeling stressed or frustrated. Members may have to take on multiple roles and more responsibility, as there are less people to do the work.

New Members

When a new member joins an existing group, the current members might expect that nothing will change. However, a new member can increase uncertainty creating feelings of awkwardness in the group. This is because the new person is uncertain what to expect from the group members and the existing members are uncertain what to expect from the new member. The group will go through the process of self-disclosure and behavioral reinforcement to reduce uncertainty and develop trust, so that they can work more effectively with each other.

A new member brings with them their past experiences from other groups, so they may expect to do things the way they did before. Even if their role in the group is assigned like in a job description, they will need to negotiate their own place within the group through the process of behavioral reinforcement.

All group members go through the process of behavior reinforcement. When we communicate or do something, we receive one of three responses from others. We are either accepted, rejected, or ignored. If we receive positive feedback we feel accepted and are likely to repeat it. If it is repeated enough times, it becomes part of the group's structure. This is how roles, norms, rules, and leaders are formed in groups and organizations.

An established group may have procedures to bring in new members. Some groups have restrictive guidelines for approving new members, while others are happy to have anyone join. Some groups allow new members to simply show up if they want to join, which means that they may have little or no control over who is a member. Other groups have a process or criteria for accepting new members.

Consideration should be given to a person's experience, education, expertise, and ability to accomplish the task. Consideration should also be given to their group skills like their ability to work in a group with others, their commitment to the group, how they make decisions, and how they deal with tension and conflict. These skills are important because they determine how well a new member will work with others in the group.

No group remains the same, existing members leave and new members join. The more formal the group and the higher the turnover, the more helpful it is for groups to develop a way for new members to smoothly join the group. A new member should be given time to get to know the other group members on a personal level. This helps fulfill the task as well as social needs of the group and its members.

**Even in groups where there are written rules,
there are often unwritten rules that members must follow.**

In formal groups, like a business, new members may go through an orientation or training program to learn about their group or organization. Whether you are a part of a group that just formed or are a new member in an existing group, these are some characteristics of an effective group member.

• Participate. Be there, show up for meetings, be on time, and stay until the end. The most frequent complaint people have about other group members is that they arrive late, leave early, or just don't show up. This behavior can be perceived as a lack of respect for others and their time.

• Contribute. Groups are about sharing resources in order to get things done. Every group has tasks that need to be accomplished so you need to contribute time, energy, expertise, experience, attention, or material resources to help the group.

• Be courteous to other group members and show them respect to receive it in return. This creates a positive environment so that the group can work together.

• Be prepared. Do your homework and be prepared for meetings and activities. Not being prepared undermines the effectiveness of the group and wastes time for the members who are prepared.

• Do your fair share. Groups need to get things done and effective groups share tasks fairly between group members. Group members are willing to pick up the slack when necessary. Know what is expected of you and fulfill those responsibilities because people don't like having to do the work of others.

• Follow the rules. All groups have rules. Get to know what they are and follow them because without rules, the group could not function effectively.

• Support others. One of the reasons for joining a group is to get support. Support the other group members because you want them to support you. If they don't support you, look for another group that will.

• Acknowledge the contributions of other members. Respond positively to their ideas and agree with them when possible. Support the group process to make and implement decisions.

• Be fair, objective, and open minded. Consider what others have to say. Consider new ideas and new information. Consider the possibility that you might not always be right about everything all the time.

• Be ethical. Avoid being overly critical of others, do not play politics, do not have hidden agendas, and do not act in your own self interest. The group exists for the good of everyone not just to benefit one person or a select few.

• Help the group achieve its desired outcomes. You can do this by putting the group's needs above your own. You can keep the group moving forward to accomplish its task by contributing, by evaluating information on its merits, and encouraging the group to make good decisions that will benefit everyone.

• Help individual members to fulfill their needs and wants. By helping others get what they want, hopefully they will help you get what you want. If you help them and they don't help you in return, look for another group that will.

Difficult Members

While these are characteristics of an effective group member, not all group members will have them. Sometimes a member can become detrimental to the group.

• They may avoid work, be overly negative, criticize others, or upset the group's progress.
• They may want attention because they feel that no one listens to them or they do not have a say in the group.
• Their perceptions may not be meeting their expectations.
• They may feel that they are not getting fair rewards for their contributions.
• They may feel that the group is going in the wrong direction, making bad decisions, or is not doing what they expect.
• Their problems can become a problem for the entire group.

These are options when working with difficult group members. Start with the more informal approaches and progress to the more formal ones as needed.

1. Talk to them about what's bothering them. Perhaps the group is not meeting their expectations or fulfilling their needs and wants. They may feel that they are contributing, but not receiving what they expect in return.

2. Talk to other group members who may be willing to speak with them about their problem. Sometimes people just want to vent and have someone listen to them.

147

3. During a meeting ask members if they have any problems. Hopefully the disruptive member will talk about their problem. Keep the discussion on track, so it doesn't break down into chaos because everyone may feel they have something they want to complain about.

4. The group may need to let them know what they are doing in a descriptive, nonjudgmental way and give them a chance to respond. The difficult member may not be aware that they are causing problems and may be willing to change. Doing this gives notice that their behavior is disruptive.

5. Since they have been told their behavior is disruptive, if they become disruptive again ask them directly what is bothering them. Try to address their concerns, but inform them that the group has rules and ask them to not behave in this manner or the rules will be enforced.

6. Get outside support. Many groups have connections to groups or organizations that provide assistance in dealing with disruptive members. Businesses often have a committee that reviews employee behavior, or may offer counseling or support.

7. If this doesn't work, the group may need to remove the member as quickly and pleasantly as possible. How this is done depends upon the rules of the group. Groups and organizations often have rules for these situations. If your group does not, consider making some.

These approaches give you options, but things may not go well. Some people become defensive lashing out at other members, perhaps even threatening them. There are some situations where the only solution is to remove the disruptive member for the good of the group.

By pursuing other options first, the group has made an effort to resolve the situation before taking punitive action. If the group decides to remove a difficult member, they must have a united front because if there is dissent within the group, it could split the group making it unable to function.

If the difficult member is not removed from the group, the other members might become frustrated or unhappy with the group. This is necessary for the good of the group because if a difficult group member is allowed to stay, it can undermine the other members' commitment to the group and good members may leave.

In a business, if an employee is having problems, they should first be given a chance to correct them. Being fired should never be a surprise to someone.

No one should ever be summoned to an office and summarily fired. It's demeaning and it reflects badly on the organization and the person doing the firing. It increases uncertainty undermining employee commitment and investment because they might be let go too.

Try these options first.

1. Meet with the employee to tell them what needs improvement, what they need to do, the time frame to do it, and the consequences if they don't.

2. If they do these things, let them know they have improved. If they don't, inform them where they are deficient. Give them a deadline to make improvements or they will be let go.

3. If they still do not remedy the situation, then they need to be let go or they could undermine the organization. Meet with them again. Give them the reasons for their dismissal. Be truthful, but tactful, avoid clichés or platitudes. Express regret for having to do this and wish them well. Avoid making it personal or drawn out.

It can also be difficult when a member voluntarily leaves the group. If a group is having some of its members leave, the remaining members may feel abandoned or rejected. This is because our self-concept is to some extent connected to the groups we belong to based on how the other members communicate with us.

Leaving a group or organization can be more difficult than joining it because when we leave we often leave friendships behind, give up benefits, and make changes that increase uncertainty reducing stability and predictability. We may feel a sense of loss and even go through a period of mourning.

If we leave to join a new group, we will go through the process of behavior reinforcement all over again by getting used to a new set of norms, rules, and getting to know a new group of people.

People leave a group either because they choose to or because they have to leave. People may choose to leave groups because the group is no longer meeting their needs and wants, they are looking for a change, or the group has changed from what they expected.

People leave groups because they retire, move away, are fired, or they have to leave. We should expect to leave groups and to have other people leave the groups that we are in. While knowing that leaving groups is inevitable and unavoidable, it doesn't always make it any easier.

**Groups are attractive because they have the
resources and ability to fulfill many of our needs and wants.**

Group needs.

Groups save us time and effort by fulfilling many of our needs on a continuous basis. Without groups, each time we had a need or want to be fulfilled we would have to look for a way to fulfill it.

For example, we belong to groups to have an income, which fulfills our monetary needs. If we did not belong to a group by having a job, every time we needed money we would spend time and energy looking for something to do to make it.

How groups use resources to fulfill needs and wants is a source of tension.

These are some sources of tensions and options for alleviating them.

• Decision making. Groups can get caught up in tensions between competing interests. Members need to make decisions as a group, however, they also make decisions as individuals creating tension between the needs of the group and its members. Groups can take longer to make decisions than individuals, which can create tension. To avoid unnecessary tension, groups should develop a process to solve problems and make decisions.

• Conflict. No two people see everything exactly the same, so all members can potentially see things differently causing conflict. The more members, the more sources of disagreement and tension. This is why groups should develop a process to deal with conflicts before they occur, so they can be resolved when they do.

• Pressures to conform. Groups exert pressure on their members to conform to their group norms. While rules are important to keep the group together, they could also keep it from being effective. By being aware of this, groups can develop norms of behavior that keeps the group functioning effectively.

• Costs and rewards. Groups provide benefits that come at a cost. The difference between our perceptions of what we contribute compared to our expectations of what we receive affects our satisfaction and commitment to the group. If we feel that we are making fair contributions and receiving fair benefits, we feel a sense of satisfaction that can increase our commitment.

However, if we feel we are contributing more and receiving less than our fair share, we are likely to become dissatisfied reducing our commitment. If we are too dissatisfied, we may look to join another group.

If enough members feel this way it can undermine the effectiveness of the group creating tension and conflict. Groups can avoid unnecessary tension by encouraging its members to clearly communicate their perceptions and expectations. Balancing responsibilities and rewards can help group members feel that they are receiving fair returns for fair contributions.

• Individuality and affiliation. When we join a group we give up some of our freedom by letting the group make some decisions for us. We do this because groups provide benefits like monetary, social, and status rewards. In exchange, we give up some of our time, energy, and freedom. This gives the group power to control our behavior in the group through norms, rules, and patterns of communicating.

Groups can help alleviate tension between members and the group by clearly communicating the group's expectations for behavior and allowing for some degree of individual differences within the rules of the group. They can have group members come up with some of the rules because people are more likely to support rules when they have a say in making them.

• Time. Groups take time to meet, make decisions, and get things done. How members perceive the group is using their time can be a source of tension especially if they think others are wasting it. This can cause them to become impatient or unhappy with the group. Groups can reduce tension by being aware of how members feel their time is being used. If members feel the group is wasting their time, they will become dissatisfied reducing their commitment or may leave the group.

• Individual personalities. While we choose many of the groups we belong to, we cannot always choose who else belongs to these groups. Sometimes members get along while other times they can be at odds with one another. Some members may try to dominate or control the group for their own gain, while other members may hold back or withdraw.

If a group is not accomplishing its tasks, members may become unhappy and not contribute making the group less effective. To reduce this tension, a group should develop behavioral norms, methods of decision making, clearly defined roles, and other structural mechanisms to help the group achieve its desired outcomes. This can help to keep overbearing members at bay and encourage those who may hold back to contribute. A group should create expectations that all members will work together for the good of the group.

• Individual responsibility. Groups have a shared sense of responsibility and each group member should assume responsibility for their actions within the group. Differences in perceptions and expectations can lead to tension or conflict over who is responsible for what tasks. Members may try to avoid taking responsibility by claiming it was not up to them or that others were responsible for what happened.

In order to avoid this, clearly communicate who is responsible for doing what tasks and have a contingency plan if things do not go as expected. While one person may cause a problem, the other members may bear the consequences for what that member does, even if they had nothing to do with it.

• Group change. Group members can have different expectations about change. Some people join a group hoping it will never change and others join so they can change it. This can create tension between those trying to change the group and those who resist change. In order for any change to be successful, members need to be comfortable with change or they may work to undermine it. The more people feel something is at stake or that the change will cause them to lose something they have invested, the more they may work against it to try to stop it.

So, it's helpful to communicate the benefits of change and to have a process where everyone can contribute. When people have something to gain and they have a say in making the decisions that affect them, they are more likely to support them and see that they are successfully implemented.

• Desired outcomes. We join groups to accomplish things that we cannot do as individuals. Ideally, our individual desired outcomes should be compatible with those of the group, however, this is not always the case. It is more common for a group's desired outcome to come into conflict with those of individual members.

There is a natural tendency for members to put their own needs, wants, and desired outcomes above those of the group. If the group is not meeting their needs and wants they are more likely to work for their own benefit rather than for the group.

This can be damaging to the group because if everyone pursued their own objectives, the group might not accomplish its tasks.

The group's desired outcomes must come first, if members do whatever they want, there is no longer any purpose to having a group.

However, if individual needs and wants are not fulfilled, tension is created and people might leave the group in order to have them fulfilled elsewhere. Putting group goals over your own creates interdependence between individuals because the outcome affects all of its members.

For example, a sports team either wins or loses. All members win or lose together collectively as a group. Because the outcome for all members is dependent upon one another, there is an incentive to work together.

This creates interdependence where the desired outcomes of all the members are tied together. While not all groups have such a clear cut outcome, when a group is successful all members should benefit.

Group satisfaction.

How satisfied we are with the groups we belong to is based, in part, on how well we perceive our expectations are being met. We have expectations about what we contribute as well as receive from the group. If our perception is close to our expectations, we are likely to be happy. If our perceptions don't meet our expectations, we can become unhappy, frustrated, and may even leave the group.

To avoid this happening, it's helpful to check your perceptions and expectations. We all have perceptions and expectations about how well our needs and wants are being met by the groups we belong to, however, it is easy to be unaware of how these can motivate our behavior.

For each group you belong to, write down your needs and wants. Then rank them in order of importance. Write down your expectations for yourself, other members, and the group. Then write down your perceptions about how well your expectations, needs, and wants are being met.

We think that we may know how we feel, but writing it down makes you think it through. Having a list gives you a starting point to determine what things are working in each group and which things could use improvement. Once you know what they are you can develop ways to improve them.

For each group and organization you belong to it can be helpful to consider the following questions.

- What are my needs and wants from my group?
- What are my group member's needs and wants from our group?
- What are my desired outcomes from my group?
- What are my group member's desired outcomes from our group?
- What are my perceptions of my group?
- What are my group members' perceptions of our group?
- What are my expectations about myself and the other members of my group?
- What are my group members' expectations of our group?
- Are those expectations being met? How can they be better met?
- Is there a gap between my perceptions and expectations that could cause tension?
- How does my group communicate, make decisions, solve problems, and allocate resources?
- What are my group's rules, roles, rituals, traditions, and norms of behavior?

The purpose of these questions is to think about important aspects of the group. These questions are not meant to be a comprehensive list, but rather a place to begin. They can help to give you a better idea of what to expect from groups.

This approach could be used to evaluate a group's effectiveness to help each member to better understand how they perceive themselves, the other members, and their group.

Think about what it would be like if you no longer belonged to any groups. Jesus spent forty days fasting in the desert. Buddha was thought to have spent forty nine days sitting under a tree to find spiritual enlightenment.

If you could get away from all the groups you belong to for a while, what would you do? What new insights could you gain about yourself, others, and the world around you?

Would you read, develop a new skill, travel, or sit under a tree?

Chapter 13
Be in Charge, Leaders and Leadership

A leader is a specific role that is created within a group. It can be the most important role because a leader has power and influence over the other members of a group. A leader is responsible for managing the group, assigning tasks, regulating norms, allocating resources, and enforcing the rules.

Groups and organizations have different types of leaders that gain their position by a variety of means. These are some of the most common types of leaders.

• Task leader. They keep the group together so that it can accomplish its tasks and achieve its desired outcomes. They see that all members have something to do and that they do it. They can be appointed, promoted, a founder of the group, or are selected through behavioral reinforcement.

• Social leader. They help maintain the social well-being of the group by promoting social activities and interpersonal relationships between members. They help members to fit in, maintain member satisfaction, and encourage commitment to the group.

• Natural leader. This person becomes a leader through the process of behavioral reinforcement. They are chosen by the other group members to lead the group. They may not necessarily be the task or appointed leader.

• Appointed leader. Groups may have a leader who is appointed or designated by someone outside the group. For example, a work group may have a leader appointed by the boss. They may still need to go through the process of behavioral reinforcement to become a leader to be effective.

• Founder. Groups and organizations are created by an individual or group of people. The founders often have special status in the group because they have been in the group the longest. In a company they often become the president or CEO. Over time they become part of the group's culture and history.

• Power leader. This is a person who uses power, influence, and control over others to become a leader. Power can come from a person's experience, expertise, charisma, or by force. They may gain power by promising group members benefits in exchange for their position. Some leaders may use force, coercion, threats, manipulation, or relationships with other influential people to gain a position of leadership.

• Motivational leader. This person becomes a leader based upon their power of persuasion and their ability to motivate people to follow them.

• Charismatic leader. These people are attractive to others and are often good speakers making them persuasive, which motivates people to follow them.

• Situational leader. There are times when groups face unusual circumstances like a crisis. A person becomes a leader because of their skills or expertise in facing a particular situation, solving a problem, or resolving a crisis.

• Visionary leader. People will follow a leader who presents a vision of the future that looks better than today. These leaders can be particularly effective when people are facing difficult times or a crisis and want things to get better.

• Spiritual leader. Authority is based upon appealing to people's spiritual or religious beliefs in a higher power. This form of leadership is attractive when people feel uncertain about other forms of leadership or are looking for answers in life.

• Coaching. Some leaders approach leadership like sports. They might act like a coach who provides their experience and expertise to help the team. A variation of the coach is the facilitator, someone outside the group who has experience or expertise to help the group facilitate their development or complete a task.

• Manager. A manager manages people compared to a leader who leads them.

• Teacher. Leaders may characterize themselves as teachers helping others to learn how to solve problems for themselves rather than providing answers. They may see part of being a leader as educating other members.

• Military. Some leaders use a military approach, like a general leading troops into battle. This is a direct approach by giving orders that others are expected to follow.

• Legitimation. A leader must have a legitimate claim to lead others. Legitimation has been used throughout history. Royalty claimed legitimacy by bloodline, pharaohs claimed descendancy from the gods, and in a democracy leaders claim legitimacy from the will of the people. If a person becomes a leader of any other type they need to legitimize their claim to leadership, otherwise people may become disenchanted and not follow them.

Becoming a Leader

Since the leader is such an important role it can be the most difficult one for the group to fill. Not everyone wants to be a leader and only a few members are ever considered. So, leaders can be determined through the process of behavioral reinforcement

This is how behavioral reinforcement works. When we communicate or do something, we receive one of three responses from others. We are either accepted, rejected, or ignored.

If we receive positive feedback we feel accepted and are likely to repeat it. If it is repeated enough times, it becomes part of the group's structure. This is how roles, norms, rules, and leaders are formed in groups and organizations.

If we receive negative feedback, we may feel rejected. We may try a different approach and if we receive negative feedback again, we can become frustrated, so we don't do it again. It may even hurt our self-concept. If feedback is ambiguous or unclear, we may repeat it until we get either positive or negative feedback.

There is no one best way to become a group leader. Becoming a leader often depends upon gaining the support of the other group members. If you want to be a leader you have to act like one and make connections with the other group members.

These are some characteristics of leaders.

• Show up. Arrive early, stay late, and don't miss meetings. One of the simplest things you can do is show up. Few things irritate people more than someone who shows up late, leaves early, or misses meetings. To be a leader it takes commitment and dedication to the group above and beyond what is expected of other members.

• Talk. Talk appropriately contributing to the group discussion. Do not dominate the conversation, but do not hold back either. Keep what you say straightforward, easy to understand, and nonjudgmental. Leaders listen to what other people say and then know when to speak up, what to say, and when to stop talking.

• Listen. When others speak actually listen to them. Ask them questions to draw them out. Look at the big picture and don't get bogged down in excessive details or petty squabbles. Listen to what others say and then develop your own ideas to help the group achieve its desired outcomes. If you listen to them, they should listen to you in return.

• Feedback. Be warm and friendly to the other members. Provide positive feedback because it bolsters their self-concept. Be polite and supportive of other people and their ideas, so they will be supportive of you.

• Be serious. Joking around and being the center of attention may get people to laugh or like you, but they are not likely to take you seriously as a leader.

• Be informed. Do your homework, gather information, and be prepared. People who are perceived as knowledgeable have a greater chance of becoming a leader.

• Avoid taking sides. We want to support others, however, by taking sides in a conflict you may end up alienating others in the group. Instead, offer suggestions and alternatives to help them find a solution that everyone can agree on. Avoid taking positions that others may not support because leaders need support.

• Pick your battles. There will be times when you will have to take a decisive position and that can mean taking sides. The old adage, pick your battles applies here. There will be times when if you don't take a decisive position and fight for what is right others will think you are incapable of making decisions.

There's no one right way to be a leader.
Leadership depends on a leader's characteristics,
the group's tasks, its members, and their desired outcomes.

Styles of leadership.

Approaches vary from hands on to delegating, from analytical to creative, from flexible to structured, and from democratic to authoritarian. Effective leaders are aware of their own leadership style and can utilize a variety of options depending on their circumstances.

• Hands-on leadership is when a leader is involved in many aspects of a group including decision making and helping members with the group's tasks. A hands-on approach can be helpful when a leader is engaged in what is going on in the group. However, being too hands on could be perceived as interference or lack of trust in the other members.

• Delegating authority is when a leader puts other people in charge of getting certain tasks done. Leaders can use this style to give group members more responsibility and more of a say in what happens in the group. Doing this can help to develop their leadership abilities. However, some leaders might use this as an excuse to not do the work themselves.

• Analytical leadership looks at things from a scientific perspective, sometimes quantifying things by putting numbers on them so they can be measured. For example, productivity can be measured in numbers or percentages, which can be useful for comparison. However, it can overlook the human aspects of the group.

• Creative leadership breaks out of conventional structures based upon the specific circumstances. Creativity helps to look at a situation in a new way to find different solutions. However, this style can be perceived as lacking structure. Some members might lose confidence in the ability of the group to accomplish its tasks.

• Democratic leadership lets everyone have a say in decision making. This encourages members to contribute to the group. However, decisions may take longer and may be more difficult to reach. There is a greater possibility of disagreement and conflict slowing down the group creating tensions and divisions between members.

• Authoritarian leadership controls group members giving them very little say because decisions are made by the leader. This style of leadership works when a task needs to be done quickly or decisively, or when there are few options and the outcome is clear like in emergency situations. However, this style of leadership can motivate members to withdraw and not contribute reducing their commitment to the group.

While these represent some styles of leadership, most leaders utilize a combination of them depending on the circumstances. At times they may use authority to make quick decisions for the good of the group. Other times they lead based upon group consensus and support.

Leaders need to provide structure for stability, but also be flexible enough to change based on the circumstances. Some problems need to be looked at analytically while others need a creative solution.

**A group should not exist to support their leader,
a leader should support the members of a group, so they can get the job done.**

Functions of a Leader

• Leaders reduce uncertainty. People join groups to reduce uncertainty and leaders can help the group stabilize its structure, rules, roles, norms, and other ways of doing things. They help the group to achieve its desired outcomes.

• Leaders allocate resources to fulfill group members' needs and wants. They instill confidence in the group by being supportive, helpful, fair, and by doing what they say they are going to do.

• Leaders provide information, allocate resources, delegate responsibility, and assign tasks so members can work more effectively. They help the group make decisions by encouraging everyone to contribute to the group. They help the group solve problems, work out disagreements, and resolve conflicts. They do this to encourage member satisfaction and commitment to the group.

• Leaders facilitate shared meaning. They encourage self-disclosure, so members feel comfortable with one another enabling them to work together more effectively. They can help members feel that they are making a contribution and are valued as part of the group. They help members feel like they fit in with the group and introduce new members to others making them feel comfortable.

Leaders can lead the group in rituals and traditions that share meaning in the group. They can help members understand the history and significance of the group and what it means to be a member.

• Leaders communicate the big picture and a vision of the future, so that group members know where they fit in, where they are going, and what to expect in the future.

• Leaders encourage investment. It is important to create and maintain the stability of the group by having rules and fairly enforcing them. They help create an atmosphere of trust so members can invest their time and other resources in the group.

Leaders see that everyone benefits from the group and receives fair rewards for fair contributions. They help encourage longevity of the group for its members, so they are comfortable being a member of the group for long periods of time. They maintain connections outside the group to help bring in information and other resources the group needs.

• Leaders encourage members to participate in decision making, so they have a feeling of participating in the group process. Leaders set an example, so other members put the interests of the group above their own. They give credit to other members and reward them for what they do.

• Leaders don't seek out credit for themselves, but share it with others. They bring out leadership qualities in others by helping them to develop their competence and bolster their confidence. They are not threatened by the successes of others, but compliment the accomplishments and achievements of other members.

• Leaders help fulfill needs and wants. We join groups to fulfill our needs and wants. Since leaders allocate benefits they can provide rewards for members who do well and penalties for those who break the rules.

• Leaders help increase member satisfaction and increase commitment by making the group attractive. They recruit new members and help them to learn the rules of the group so they will fit in.

• Leaders can shape perceptions and expectations. Everyone has expectations about what a leader should be and what they should do. Leaders can clearly communicate their perceptions so that group members have realistic expectations of them. Leaders can provide current and accurate information about the group and what is happening to keep the perceptions and expectations of their members in line with reality.

All too often there is a tendency for leaders to portray things better than they really are, so that others will like them and follow them. They may do this if they are fearful that by being honest they may lose the group's support. By being truthful, but tactful they can help the group to create accurate perceptions and realistic expectations.

• Leaders can be more effective when they have an awareness of their own style of communicating, the style of their members, and the style of outsiders. They need to have an awareness of what is going on both inside the group and things going on outside the group that affects it.

• Leaders help members to solve problems, make decisions, and achieve the group's desired outcomes. They help to develop individual member's expertise, experience, education, and skills for the good of the group. They can help to create options to avoid potential problems by being proactive rather than reactive. Leaders help to develop leadership skills in others.

• Leaders communicate the big picture to the group by taking the pieces and putting them together, so that everyone knows how they fit in and how they contribute to the whole. People are more committed to groups and organizations when they understand the big picture, know how they fit in, and can see that they make a difference.

All too often we do not see the big picture or know where we fit in creating a sense that what we do does not matter. By seeing the big picture, people can feel that they are part of something bigger than themselves.

This can help them to see what they do matters and they are making a difference. This helps increase individual member's satisfaction and commitment to the group.

• Leaders communicate a vision of the future, which is a comparison of the current situation to what the group could look like in the future. It includes a course of action to achieve that vision. Leaders use vision to motivate members to contribute to the group and work together to achieve their desired outcomes.

The key to becoming an effective leader is having
an awareness of your own leadership style, skills, and abilities.
Then, having options to choose the right approach in a given situation.

In businesses and organizations, information often originates at the top where decisions are made and then filters down to the lower levels. To communicate more effectively, leaders need to get information from all levels, particularly where the work is done in order to make good decisions.

Since employees must listen to their leaders, leaders should listen to their employees to get information to improve the effectiveness of the organization. Doing this can help people to feel like they matter.

Some groups seem to get along and things go well, so we don't think much about them. Other times nothing seems to work leaving us feeling frustrated.

An effective leader can help diagnose problems and find solutions to make things more effective. They can help the group create norms, roles, rules, structures, and a social reality that will help them achieve their desired outcomes.

Chapter 14
Be Smarter in Organizations

**An organization is a group of people brought together
by common interests to achieve mutual desired outcomes.**

Organizations can create their own specialized form of social reality that shapes how we see ourselves, others, and the world around us. We are motivated to join them because they have the ability to allocate resources to help us achieve our desired outcomes and fulfill material and social needs and wants.

This gives them power to motivate and influence behavior. In many ways groups and organizations can have considerable influence over us.

Organizations have many of the characteristics of a group, but are generally larger.
*   They can be made up of many smaller groups joined by connections making up networks that regulate the flow of information and resources.
*   They tend to be more formal than groups with well defined rules, structures, and boundaries.
*   They have tasks and desired outcomes that members are expected to fulfill based upon specialized roles.
*   They often have centralized power with clear lines of authority, levels of management, and a hierarchy of importance.
*   They allocate resources, provide rewards, and extract costs giving them power and social control over their members.
*   They have norms of behavior that are regulated by rules enforced with rewards and punishments.

Organizational structure.

In order to function effectively, organizations need structure. Structure consists of different types of connections between its members. It also includes an organization's rules, roles, and norms of behavior. Organizations need to develop structure so that they can accomplish their tasks and achieve their desired outcomes.

These are some of the structures that can be found in organizations.

• Power structure. Organizations have official power structures with power concentrated at the top flowing down through the organization. Power is having the authority over others to regulate their behavior. However, people can hold power at any level because of their skills, knowledge, connections, influence, information, or the length of time they have been with the organization. It can be helpful to get to know the people who have power in your organization.

• Task structure. This consists of the connections between members that help them to work together to accomplish tasks and achieve their desired outcomes. Task structures include division of labor, departments, and role specialization. They let people know their responsibilities and what tasks they are expected to do. People may create their own informal structures to communicate based upon their needs and wants, common interests, and areas of expertise.

• Social structure. While the focus of an organization is to accomplish tasks, social relationships can be just as important. The social structure is who communicates informally with whom about things that are not task related. Developing social relationships reduces uncertainty, so that members can invest their time and other resources in the organization and in each other.

• Time structure. Time is a valuable resource in organizations and how they use it communicates their priorities and what they value. This includes how members organize their day, week, and year. Do they spend their time in meetings, at their desk, or with customers and clients? It also includes social uses of time for rituals and traditions like coffee breaks and important days like holidays. Time is prioritized and tasks organized based upon their importance to the organization.

• Space structure. Organizations are not just comprised of people, they also include buildings, offices, and other types of space. How organizations utilize space can tell a lot about what is valued and how people communicate with one another. Since physical space is often valuable, organizations make decisions about how to organize and allocate their space based upon their values. Larger offices in nicer locations are often given as a reward for service to the organization.

Spatial structure is not just physical, it can be psychological. People often have an area of responsibility or expertise like their turf or territory, which they are likely to protect from incursions by others. People are more likely to communicate with others that are in close physical proximity, like the adjoining work spaces as well as psychological proximity, like working on similar tasks.

**In order to fit in, it can be helpful to communicate
the right messages. While we might focus on what we say,
much of what others perceive about us is communicated nonverbally.**

These are some ways we communicate nonverbally in organizations.

• Time. How people use time communicates their values and priorities. Different groups have different values when it comes to utilizing time. For some, punctuality is valued above all else. In others, getting things done is valued. If someone is working on a project they may continue to work rather than taking time out for a meeting. They may place value on how people spend social time including coffee breaks, lunch, and other activities like participating in sports or volunteering in the community.

• Space. Space means not only physical space, but also territory or turf. Organizations have to place their people in specific locations, buildings, and next to other people, which communicates what's important to them. Consider how offices are physically arranged like who is next to whom, which ones are open or closed, and what people are accessible or blocked by gatekeepers like receptionists or security.

People in organizations often stake out their own territory and defend it against intrusions by others. Territory can be seen as allocation of resources, use of space, influence over others, and duties or responsibilities.

• Symbols. Organizations have symbols that people invest with meaning. The most common are an organization's name, colors, and logo, which are used as a form of identity management. Organizations have other symbols that members invest with meaning like badges, uniforms, or artwork. This can include the type of building they occupy, where it is located, how offices and public spaces are decorated, and what people choose to put in their offices.

• Appearance. How we look can be important because of what it communicates to others. Organizational norms can determine how people dress, how they do their hair and makeup, and what accessories they wear including jewelry or watches.

Appearance communicates information about a person's job, values, even their income. Many professions have uniforms that communicate their job, position, or rank like the police and military. Groups and organizations use appearance and clothing like uniforms to communicate expertise, competence, and authority.

Organizational Climate

**Organizational climate is the emotional tone
of how people interact with one another in an organization.**

Organizational climate is important because it affects the state of mind of individual members and how well they can do their job. While it is mostly psychological in nature, it is communicated through the social interaction of people, so it can affect their behavior.

Organizational climate is an important part of an organization because it can make us feel good about ourselves. A positive climate makes an organization a fun place to be, motivating people to want to be a part of it. A negative climate can reduce an individual's commitment to the organization, so they feel less satisfied making them more likely to leave.

Organizational climate is important because it affects the ability of its members to work together and accomplish its desired outcome. This is because climate has an influence on each member's perceptions and expectations of themselves, others, and the organization.

These are some elements of organizational climate.

• Emotional. Most of the time we are in a generally good mood, so we don't think about how we feel until something happens that puts us in a bad mood. People can pick up on the emotional intensity of others and transfer those emotions through the connections between people spreading them through the organization.

• Openness. Climate includes how open people are with one another. They may share information freely, openly, and honestly. Conversely, a climate may be restrictive so people don't say what's on their mind. The degree of openness in an organization depends on how people use filters to keep information from getting to others particularly those at the top who make decisions.

• Adaptability. Climate can fluctuate between strict and flexible. Some organizations have strict standards that members are expected to follow giving them little choice, like a sports team where the desired outcome is to win. Others are flexible where choice and creativity are valued. An organization has to find a balance between strict and flexible that helps them accomplish their desired outcomes.

• Patterns of communicating. People tend to follow familiar patterns of communicating, which are reoccurring patterns we use to talk to one another. These patterns create climates that can be positive or negative, warm or cold, and friendly or formal. This is determined by the tone of communicating between them.

This can include their appearance, nonverbal body language, facial expressions, posture, and tone of voice. Most of the time these patterns are meant to create a positive climate, but if they are overly negative it can form a climate that undermines their effectiveness and commitment.

• The weather. The climate in an organization can be described like the weather. It can be sunny, cloudy, or stormy. Positive climates can be characterized as warm and sunny, and negative ones cold and stormy. These climates can travel through the communicating networks in an organization like storms travel across the countryside. Sometimes you can do something to improve them. Other times, just like the weather, there's not much you can do other than taking cover and riding them out until they pass.

People have expectations about what type of climate they need to do their best work. This is often based upon their past experiences and personal preferences. Some people prefer a climate that is informal, fun, warm, friendly, and open to new ideas and information. Others may prefer a more fixed, formal, and structured climate that values tradition.

If people fit in with the organizational climate, they are more likely to feel comfortable as a part of the organization. If the climate is meeting their needs, it can increase their satisfaction and commitment. If a member does not fit in with the organizational climate they can feel uncomfortable, not accepted, or that their needs are not being met. They may feel like an outsider even though they are in the organization. This can be a source of tension or conflict undermining the effectiveness of the organization.

These approaches can be used to improve an organization's climate.

1. Awareness. It's easy to be unaware of why we feel the way we do, so we may end up being upset or unhappy, but don't know why. How we feel may come from being around other people because we can pick up the emotions of others. Being aware of how we feel and where our feelings come from can help us to improve the climate around us.

2. Appreciate. We can create a positive climate by considering how we would like to be treated and then treating others that way. We can be considerate of others and their point of view by looking for things we have in common.

3. Attention. People may get upset because others don't pay attention to them. Pay attention to others by listening and providing feedback. We can belong to an organization where no one says anything to us. When people are friendly and pay attention to one another they feel like they belong. This affirms their value as a member of the organization.

4. Acknowledgment. People may feel that they are not given credit for what they do. Acknowledgment is a strong social reward, so thanking them for their work can improve an organization's climate. Organizations can develop rituals to provide recognition and rewards to its members for their contributions.

5. Agreement. This is one of the strongest social rewards that people can provide because it shows their opinions are valued by others. When we agree with someone, we create common ground. Finding some area of agreement can reduce the emotional intensity of a negative climate. We can agree with the other person's perceptions and feelings validating their self-concept without necessarily validating their position or agreeing with everything.

6. Disagreement. We can't agree with everyone all the time. There needs to be some disagreement in order to test and evaluate ideas to make good decisions. Disagree in a positive way by being truthful but tactful, be descriptive rather than characterizing things as good or bad, and consider how you would want to be told the same information. Focus on the situation rather than on the individual.

7. Adjustment. If a negative climate is harming the organization, direct intervention may be needed. Ask others how they feel about the situation. Determine the cause, which could be from a lack of resources, lack of support, lack of cooperation, feeling overworked, or a lack of fairness. By getting things out in the open a solution is easier to find.

Organizational Culture

Organizational culture is the reoccurring patterns of communicating and behavior between individuals in an organization.

Organizational culture can be like the culture of a country. It can include its history, language, customs, rituals, and social reality. This can make becoming a new member of an organization feel like going to a foreign country. It's helpful for members of an organization to know about its culture, so they feel like they fit in.

While an organizational climate can change to reflect the emotional intensity of the moment, organizational culture changes more slowly over time. An organization's culture is formed when the organization is created. It develops in one of two ways. It can grow spontaneously through the natural interaction of its members through the process of behavioral reinforcement. Or, it can be created and developed intentionally to achieve specific desired outcomes.

However, when a culture is imposed on an organization, the members may try to create their own informal culture. By understanding how culture works, organizations can have options to develop a culture that is the most effective for them.

The most common way that people learn about an organization's culture is by experiencing it for themselves. This can take some time and they may make mistakes that can cause unnecessary tension. Organizations can make this process easier by providing a means to inform their members about how their culture works.

These options can help you learn about an organization's culture.

• Awareness. Practically everything has the potential to communicate something. This includes how people talk, behave, dress, what they have in their offices, even the cars they drive. A good way to learn about an organization's culture is to observe how others communicate in both formal and informal networks. For example, who communicates with whom, about what, under what circumstances, where, and in what ways.

• Power. Power is the ability to get things done and who has it is not always who you might think it is. A person may have the appearance of power, but they may not have very much. A person who may have a position that doesn't seem significant may be influential within the organization. Often the people who can get things done are those who have been there a long time because they know how the culture works.

• Getting things done. Observe how things get done. People are constantly making decisions, so look at what criteria they use to make them. Determine what needs and wants people have and how you might be able to help fulfill them. Observe how others communicate, who they connect with, and how. For example, an email or phone message may not get answered, but people may talk to you informally over coffee. Knowing how others get things done can help you to know how to communicate to achieve your desired outcome.

• What arguments work. Notice what methods of persuasion work and which ones don't. The people who make decisions have their own needs and wants, so some arguments won't work no matter how valid they may be. It's helpful to know their needs and wants, and criteria for making decisions. For example, an organization may approve proposals that cut costs or involves health and safety issues.

You can learn how to do this by finding out how the last decisions that were approved were presented. Look at what arguments, evidence, and methods of reasoning were successful. Knowing what proposals were turned down can help you know what not to do. By knowing this you can tailor your message to increase the likelihood of it being favorably received.

• Get advice. It can be helpful to find a person who has been in the organization for some time and knows how things work who would be willing to help you and give you advice. Start slow by getting to know them through self-disclosure by sharing appropriate information to reduce uncertainty about yourself. Test the usefulness of any advice to be sure it works, because people sometimes give bad advice.

• Observe others. Watch how people behave, how they act, how they dress, and how they organize their space and time. Notice who spends time with whom, when, and under what circumstances. Listen to how they communicate with one another and the stories they tell.

• Networks. Who communicates with whom will tell you about the communicating networks and informal structures within the organization. Observing how people behave and interact with one another will tell you about their norms. How they dress can tell you something about their attitudes and values, such as if they are formal or casual.

• Observe things around you. Is the décor conservative or innovative, inexpensive or opulent? People surround themselves with objects and symbols that they invest with meaning giving them value, so it can be helpful to understand what these objects mean. For example, if everyone has pictures of their family on display, family values could be important to the organization.

• Courtesy. This is an important part of a culture because it affects how members communicate with each other and the public. Courtesy is more than just being polite or having good manners, it is an attitude that people have towards one another. It affects behavior because people are encouraged to be thoughtful and considerate, and show respect for others. There is a culture of civility and graciousness. It encourages an organizational climate that is cordial, warm, and friendly making it a pleasant place to work, that can increase satisfaction and commitment.

Organizational Change

**Times change, people change, and technology changes,
so organizations must keep up with change or risk going under.**

These are options to help facilitate change in organizations.

• Utilize the law of uncertainty. People are more likely to change when their perception of the current situation increases uncertainty making them uncomfortable. Portray change as reducing uncertainty to make things more stable and secure. If uncertainty about change is reduced, people are more likely to accept it.

• Utilize the law of shared meaning. People are more likely to change to preserve their values or uphold traditions that create stability and security. A common argument against change is that it is contrary to common values. Using tradition legitimizes change because it is based on common values and beliefs.

• Utilize the law of investing. People may fear losing what they have, so reassure them that their investment will not be lost, but rather will have greater value after the change. They are more likely to support change if they have the perception that their investment today will payoff with greater returns tomorrow.

• Utilize small changes. There is a certain amount of change that people will accept. After that, uncertainty increases and they are motivated to resist it. They are more likely to accept small incremental changes over time, than a big change all at once. Once they are comfortable with a small change, additional ones can be added until the entire change has been implemented.

• Utilize needs and wants. Even though people join organizations to have their needs and wants fulfilled, it is unlikely that they will all be fulfilled. So, present change as a means to better fulfill them. People often feel that they should be doing better and if change can help them to do that, they will be more open to it.

• Utilize the rules. People are more likely to resist change if it violates the rules. Encourage change by using existing rules. Afterwards the rules can be changed.

• Utilize influential members. Social reality is negotiated in organizations by its members in an ongoing process allowing opportunities for change. Influential members who are held in high esteem can utilize behavioral reinforcement by sending positive messages and using their influence to convince others to change.

• Utilize rewards and incentives to encourage members to change and impose costs or punishments on those who won't. Change can be encouraged by providing material and social rewards for those who support it. Have members participate, when they feel a part of the decision making process, they are more likely to see that decisions are successfully implemented.

Chapter 15
Be Smarter at Problem Solving and Decision Making

Imagine it's a typical day and your three children are fighting over the same toy. The fighting has been going on for some time now and it's getting quite loud, so you have finally had enough. What do you do?

A natural tendency might be to go over and take the toy away from them. Congratulations, you made a decision. Unfortunately, the problem has not been solved. You still have three unhappy children.

Using problem solving skills you might have looked at why the children are fighting in the first place to determine how to best solve their predicament, instead of only resolving yours.

Perhaps you could find a few other toys to take their mind off this one. Perhaps there was an activity they could do or a game they could play instead. Perhaps the toy could be shared with each one having it for a specific amount of time.

You could sit down to play with all of them and the toy together until they got tired of it. Or, perhaps they are hungry or tired and need a nap. Considering what approach to take is problem solving, doing something about it is making a decision.

Decision making and problem solving are often used interchangeably because they are similar in nature. However, there is a distinct difference between making a decision and solving a problem.

It is possible to make a decision without solving a problem. Some decisions even create them. Solving problems often necessitates making a series of decisions including choosing information, establishing evaluation criteria, selecting solutions, and implementing them.

Fortunately, methods and approaches for problem solving also apply to decision making. They give you options that can be adjusted to meet your specific needs and situation.

Some of the most commonly used methods of solving problems are not necessarily the best. All too often problems are solved based upon what is cheapest, easiest, quickest, or closest to us. We are motivated to solve problems in this way because we have limited resources like time and energy to solve them.

We solve problems and make decisions every day. We do it so much we don't think about most of them because there is not much at stake. Most of the time we do not need problem solving methods to make a decision.

We have a tendency to make important decisions the same way we make simple ones. However, what works for simple decisions may not work for important ones leading to unnecessary frustration and unhappiness.

We can fall into the habit of approaching all problems the same because we have a tendency to repeat past success. If one approach is successful, we are likely to apply it to other problems, even if it doesn't work very well. We may even use this approach when it doesn't work simply because we are comfortable with it.

Decisions can be thought of as implementing solutions to problems. When we solve a problem, a decision has to be made on how to implement that solution. Sometimes decisions do not actually solve the problems they are meant to solve.

Conversely, not every decision represents a problem that needs to be solved. For example, what to wear to work or what to have for lunch is not a problem, but involves making a decision.

**Problem solving involves coming up with solutions
and decision making is selecting one of them to implement.**

Decision inhibiting inertia.

Inertia can inhibit us from making decisions. We make many decisions every day without thinking much about them, while others can be very difficult. What makes some decisions more difficult than others? When faced with a decision where there are two or more potential outcomes, we may experience inertia preventing us from choosing one. This can happen when the outcome is uncertain and choosing one precludes the others.

As long as we haven't made a decision, all potential outcomes are still possible. Once we make a decision we have only one outcome, the one we choose. For instance, we know making a decision will result in either success or failure, but we don't know which one it will be. We want success, but there is the potential for failure. Since making a decision results in either one or the other, as long as we do not decide, success is still possible.

This can create inertia preventing us from making a decision because as long as we have not made it, there is still the potential for achieving our desired outcome. Once a decision has been made our options are gone. So, the fear of not achieving our desired outcome can inhibit us from making a decision.

An example of how inertia may inhibit us can happen in dating. When we meet someone we find attractive we have to decide whether to ask them on a date or not. Once we ask them out they either say yes, which is our desired outcome or, they say no, and it's all over. Even though we could ask them again we are discouraged and less likely to do so.

Rather than risk them saying no, which could hurt our self-esteem, we might experience a kind of paralysis that prevents us from asking them because as long as we don't ask them there's still the possibility that they could say yes. This can result in an inhibiting inertia because the possibility that they say no overshadows the likelihood that they could say yes.

It is good to have a number of options to choose from in making decisions, so we do not fall into reoccurring patterns that reduce effectiveness. However, having too many options can also create decision inhibiting inertia by overwhelming our ability to process information.

Generally, we only need so much information to make an informed decision.

Too much information can overload us making the decision more difficult. Developing effective communicating skills can help us to determine what information will help us make a decision while filtering out what does not.

These are some options for effective problem solving and decision making.

• Get good information. In cooking, preparing good food takes good ingredients. Good decisions need relevant, accurate, and current information.

• Get organized. It helps to have an organized approach in gathering and using information. When more people work on a problem, it can both help and hinder reaching a successful solution.

• Get outside of yourself. We have a tendency to try to work things out ourselves and not ask for help. However, we have connections with others who can provide information and other helpful resources. Groups can seek help from outside the group.

• Get going. In working through problems there is a tendency for groups to break the work up into small pieces giving it to individuals who work on it alone. Instead, bring group members together by asking for their help and advice to make them part of the process.

• Get a process. Groups can be more effective when they develop a variety of options so they can choose the best one for the situation. Before a solution can be reached, the group has to agree on the process by which it will be reached otherwise there may be dissent over how the decision was made undermining the effectiveness of the group.

• Get to the issue. Avoid personal or past issues that are irrelevant to the problem at hand. By getting to the issue you can better understand the cause of the problem, limit its scope, and avoid problems that can derail progress preventing you from reaching a good solution.

• Get the group to step back. It's easy to get personally invested in your own solution and try to convince others to agree with you to do things your way. By having the group take a step back, it helps everyone to be objective and avoid getting personally invested in any particular solution.

• Get the right size. Balance the group to keep its size compatible to its task. More people working on a problem can bring in more resources to solve it, gather more information, and provide more points of view. However, more people means more chances for disagreement, completing tasks may take longer, and they may not make better decisions. Balance the mix of experience and expertise in the group, so members complement each other without unnecessary overlap.

Problem solving and decision making options.

The following options provide several step by step approaches for making decisions and solving problems, not only in groups and organizations, but also for individuals, relationships, and families.

There is no one best approach to making decisions and solving problems. These methods are meant as a guide, so you can choose what works best for you in your situation. They can be altered or combined as needed.

Consensus.

This is a collective decision making process in which all members generally agree on the best course of action. Depending upon what is to be decided it may be relatively easy for a group to achieve consensus.

There may be other times when consensus cannot be reached and the group needs to be prepared to use another method of decision making.

Compromise.

This option is used when everyone gives up something they want to gain something they want in order to reach a decision. Group members may accept less than they want in order to reach agreement. Depending upon what is at stake, this approach can create friction and discontent within the group. When consensus is not achievable, compromise may be the next best choice.

Majority vote.

Voting is used in situations when other forms of decision making may not be feasible or where each member's position needs to be on the record. Voting can be the least satisfactory approach because it might create divisions within the group. Members who are outvoted may feel that they no longer count or are respected in the group. They may withdraw, retaliate, or even leave the group.

The Scientific Approach

This approach applies methods used in scientific research to problem solving and decision making. It consists of a set of steps to find a solution. These steps can be changed to fit your situation in order to achieve your desired outcome.

1. Identify the source of the problem to determine its cause.
2. Determine your desired outcome for solving the problem.
3. Establish your criteria to evaluate each solution.
4. Identify possible solutions and their workability.
5. Evaluate each solution based on your criteria.
6. Select and implement the best solution.
7. Review the effectiveness of the solution.
8. If the problem is not solved, try the next best solution, continue until one works.

**You can combine or change these
steps and approaches to fit your situation.**

The Analytical Approach

This is a more flexible variation of the scientific approach.

1. Define the problem. Determine the nature of the problem and if it really exists. Sometimes what is perceived as a problem may not be much of a problem at all if given a closer look. Many times we do not get to the true source of the problem or get bogged down in extraneous issues.

2. Isolate the scope of the problem. Problems are not always as big as they seem, so narrowing its scope to determine what the issues really are can help to solve it.

3. Evaluate the cause of the problem. Collect information about possible causes. Determine what is fact and what is opinion or speculation. The better the information, the better the solution. Knowing the source can provide insight into solutions. If only symptoms are treated, the problem will likely persist.

4. Establish objective criteria to evaluate potential solutions. Having criteria will provide you with guidelines for selecting a solution. For example, a solution may need to fit a specific time frame or be cost effective. Your criteria will help you choose the best possible solutions by eliminating those that are unworkable. Having impartial criteria helps keep the outcome objective rather than based upon individual preferences or opinions.

5. Discuss possible solutions. Develop as many workable solutions as possible without being judgmental because they will be evaluated later. Be sure everyone has had a chance to contribute their ideas. If everyone does not have their say, they may feel they were left out and resist implementing the solution.

6. Use the criteria you selected to evaluate possible solutions. Rank them from best to least workable. Consider the resources that will be needed, the cost, the time to implement, and their practical workability. Consider potential consequences of each and develop criteria to evaluate its success after implementation. By waiting to evaluate solutions until now, you avoid hindering creativity and generating ideas that might not otherwise be considered.

7. Implement the solution. Once it is implemented, evaluate it based upon your predetermined criteria to determine its effectiveness. If it is not successful, look at other solutions that have been generated that can be implemented until one works. At this point, it can be helpful to evaluate the decision making process to see how well it worked. All too often after a decision is implemented there's little or no follow up to see how well it worked.

The Creative Approach

The scientific and analytical approaches use a linear, step by step method. The creative approach uses a more flexible and open method.

1. Begin by looking at similar problems that have been successfully resolved. Considering why they worked can provide inspiration for solving the new problem. It can be helpful to know what has worked and not worked in the past.

2. Ask group members to come up with as many potential solutions as possible. Set a specific amount of time to do this before you begin. As each person comes up with a possible solution, write it down where everyone can see it. Go around the group so that everyone has a chance to participate. Encourage members to modify existing solutions using them as inspiration to come up with additional ideas. The purpose is to generate as many solutions as possible no matter how unrealistic they may sound. Do not evaluate or eliminate any of the solutions.

3. When the group is finished, combine similar ideas and eliminate unworkable ones. Then critically evaluate each of them as to how well they will solve the problem.

4. Workable solutions are put in order from most to least desirable. The best solution is implemented and criteria developed to evaluate how effective it is. If it doesn't work, then move to the next best solution on the list.

The purpose of the creative approach
is to make a decision using two different methods together.

The first is to come up with as many ideas as possible. This can encourage the group to be creative by looking at the problem and solution in a new way. It encourages them to come up with solutions they might not otherwise consider. The second method is to critically evaluate the solutions to choose the best one.

The Intuitive Approach

This approach is based on the notion that people can get too close to a problem to see it clearly or objectively. They get wrapped up in specifics that prevent them from seeing the big picture. Our mind can become overloaded, so it can be beneficial to take a break by getting away from the problem and thinking about something else for a while. Then we can take a fresh look at it later.

It works like the perception process where we select, organize, and interpret information. It can take time to process new information, so by getting away from the problem and doing something different, our mind is cleared and it can work more effectively to process information and reach a solution.

1. Begin by identifying the source of the problem or the decision to be made. The important issues are identified including the nature and scope of the problem, its causes, and potential solutions. Once all the information is gathered and understood by everyone, the group moves on to other things.

2. The group members go away and work on other tasks, so they don't work on the problem. The rationale is that when we are working intensely on a problem, our mind may become overloaded with information and we are unable to process it all. We become too close to the problem to see the big picture. It becomes so familiar that we may overlook important aspects. By setting it aside and forgetting about it for awhile we are able to relax and clear our mind, so later on we can see the problem more clearly in a new light.

3. While we are thinking about other things our subconscious mind continues to process information using the perception process to interpret and organize the new information with what we already know by giving it meaning. When the process has finished there can be a moment when a solution occurs to us. This could be an idea we hadn't thought about, and we might even see the situation in a new or different way.

4. After the group members have had time to consider the problem, they get together and present their possible solutions. Then the group works through the solutions to choose the best one based upon its workability and other criteria.

5. The best solution is implemented and evaluated for its effectiveness to determine its success. If it is not successful, there is a list of additional solutions that can be implemented without going through the whole process again.

This approach utilizes the law of shared meaning because new information has to fit in with what we already know, so that we can understand and use it. This can take some time to process especially if the new information is different than what we already know. This method is similar to the perception process of selecting, organizing, and interpreting information to make it useful to us.

When something dramatic happens we may need time to process our thoughts and feelings. If our mind does not process it, then the new information is more likely to be dismissed or rejected. When this process is over, we are more likely to utilize the new information.

The Medical Approach

There are several approaches to problem solving that are analogous to medical treatments.

• Symptoms and illness. Problems can be approached like a doctor would diagnose an illness by looking at the symptoms in order to determine its cause. When the cause has been established, a prescription and course of treatment can be developed in order to cure the illness or solve the problem.

• The holistic approach. In Eastern medicine, like acupuncture, the body is viewed as an interconnected series of systems. Acupuncture points are not necessarily located next to the part of the body they affect. For instance, many points for internal organs are found on the feet or ear.

Problems many originate in places that may not be self evident. For instance, problems with getting deliveries out on time may not be in the department that handles deliveries, but rather in the sales or information technology department.

• The allopathic approach. In Western medicine, the body is broken down into components like the circulatory or respiratory system. Each system is examined separately and becomes a specialized medical field. Illness is treated with remedies that counter the effects of the symptoms.

In this approach, a problem is broken down into smaller parts that are analyzed and resolved individually. They are then reassembled once a solution is been reached. This approach works when a problem is large and needs to be broken down into smaller pieces or systems to be solved individually in order to reach a larger solution.

The Participatory Approach

Not every member of a group contributes equally or in the same way.

In groups there may be one or two members that contribute more than the others. They may try to dominate the discussion or force their ideas on the others.

There may be some members who are quiet and hold back by not contributing as much as the others. They may have good ideas that the group never gets to hear. The participatory approach is a way to equalize the influence of all group members to encourage everyone to participate.

1. The group begins by identifying the source and scope of the problem. It identifies the decision to be made. Information is gathered about the problem including its causes and effects. Each member is given time either before or at the meeting to consider the problem and potential solutions.

2. At the meeting the members are given a few minutes to write down on a piece of paper their best possible solutions to the problem.

3. Each member is asked to rank their solutions from most to least desirable.

4. One group member serves as moderator and goes around the group asking each member to tell the group their best solution.

5. As each member tells the group their solutions, they are written down on a board in front of the group so everyone can see them.

6. The moderator goes around the group one or two more times to gather more solutions, if they are needed. Similar solutions are combined.

7. Group members are then asked to look at the list of solutions and write down three new solutions based upon the ones that are on the list.

8. The moderator goes around the group and asks each person to tell the group their best solution. They are written down on the board in front of everyone and the old list is discarded.

9. The group is then asked to discuss and evaluate the list of new solutions. The group is asked to rate the new solutions and select the best one. This process of going around the group can be repeated as many times as needed to come up with a workable solution.

A common approach is to go around the group and have everyone contribute an idea. However, while one person is explaining their idea, no one else is listening to them because they are thinking about what they are going to say.

Giving everyone a few minutes to write down their ideas before anyone speaks lets them think about what they are going to say before you begin, so they can listen to the others.

This can help everyone focus their attention on what the others have to say and actually listen to them. Having each person write a list of several ideas gives them options to choose from rather than concentrating on just one idea.

If a person before them has the same idea they can choose the next item on their list. This makes the process go smoother so no one feels like they are being put on the spot and they don't waste time trying to think of something to say.

The rationale for doing this is that people often have a preconceived notion of what they want to happen. They present their idea and then try to convince everyone else to agree with them.

The participatory approach helps everyone work together instead of having each person trying to get their idea adopted, which could divide the group.

This approach encourages everyone to utilize a truly collaborative process to create a solution together. By going around the group a few times, ideas get mixed together so no one has exclusive ownership over any one idea.

It encourages the group to come up with ideas collaboratively as a group rather than as individuals and then fight over whose idea gets chosen.

This approach gives all members a chance to contribute equally.

No members can dominate the group or withdraw from it. When everyone has a say in the process, they can feel that they have ownership of it and are more likely to support implementation of the solution.

The Long Distance Approach

This is a variation of the participatory approach that can be used when time is limited, if the group is large, is separated by long distances, or members are unable to meet together.

1. Everyone is provided information as to the nature of the problem and the decision that needs to be made.

2. When everyone has the information, they do their own research and information gathering to come up with a short list of potential solutions that are ranked in order of workability. Everyone sends their list of solutions to one designated person, like the group leader or secretary.

3. When the solutions are received, the designated person tabulates them and makes a list of the top solutions. This list can contain as many solutions as the group wants to consider. There should be at least four to eight to consider, but no more than twenty or it becomes too time consuming. The tabulated list is sent to the members.

4. Each person is asked to choose their top solution, or top three depending upon the length of the list. Their choices are ranked by which ones get the most responses.

5. At this time the group or a smaller committee can choose or vote for their top choice, which is the one that will be implemented.

6. This process can be repeated as many times as the group needs to reach a decision that is successful. The group can do this twice, but not too many more times as people may lose interest.

This process is similar to the participatory approach applying it to a large group that cannot meet all together. It uses a combination of the creative process with voting to choose a solution. It also provides a list of solutions ranked in order of preference to choose from to give the group options and alternatives in case the one chosen does not solve the problem.

The Reverse Approach

Most problem solving and decision making approaches begin with the problem and move towards finding a solution. This approach works in reverse because it starts with the solution and then works backward to the problem.

This process is used for situations where there is a clearly defined desired outcome, a fixed deadline, or other limitations.

1. Determine what the desired outcome looks like.
2. Determine the criteria for the desired outcome. For example, it needs to be workable with our current resources, meet a deadline, or be cost effective.
3. Determine what needs to happen just before the desired outcome is reached.
4. Determine what needs to happen just before the last step before the desired outcome is reached.
5. Then work backwards for each step that needs to take place in order to reach the next one.
6. Work backwards through each step until you reach the situation as it exists today.
7. Once all the steps are completed determine how well they meet the criteria you established.
8. Make a list of the resources that are needed to accomplish each step.

While this process may seem backward, it can be used for making decisions and solving problems like when building a house. If you build a house, you do not start with an empty lot, proceed to gather materials like lumber and bricks, determine the best way to assemble them, and see what you end up building.

Instead, you would draw plans of what the house will look like when it is finished. Then, you work backwards to make a materials list, set time frames for each stage, and determine the cost.

If the house needs to be completed by a specific date, a schedule can be established by working backwards from the date of completion to determine when each step needs to take place.

Chapter 16
Be Better Handling Conflict

The word conflict has been used to describe everything from disagreements to war. There are personal conflicts, sports conflicts, even armed conflicts. Conflict can be a disagreement where two or more people are at crossed purposes with incompatible objectives. It often involves some kind of struggle, perhaps even taking physical action.

For the purpose of this book, conflict takes place through verbal and nonverbal communicating between two or more people. It is more than just a difference of opinion or expression of personal preferences. It involves making decisions and taking action to achieve a resolution.

Conflict has an intensity that brings out emotional responses that can make us react less rationally resulting in unintended or undesired outcomes. So, it can be helpful to take a moment and pause to consider your desired outcome.

Is your desired outcome to escalate the situation and perhaps damage the relationship, or is it to work out a reasonable solution?

By pausing for a moment to consider your desired outcome, you can reduce the emotional intensity of the situation to increase your awareness and consider your options. By not responding to others with the same intensity, you do not give them a reason to continue to fight. Instead, they are encouraged to actually talk about the issues improving the chances for resolution.

Conflicts can vary based upon their depth and breadth. Depth is the intensity of the conflict, how deep individual feelings go, or how willing people are to dig in their heels and fight to win. The breadth of a conflict is the scope or number of issues that are involved, which can range from one to many. In determining the most effective approach, it can be helpful to determine the scope of the problem.

In order to effectively resolve a conflict, it's helpful to identify its source. Sometimes it is easily identifiable and other times it can be difficult to determine. A conflict may start with one issue and then spread to others.

Sometimes people create conflict in one area to cover up the real issues in another. They may be uncomfortable or unwilling to discuss the true source of the problem and may get upset when someone asks them about it.

To help successfully resolve a conflict, it can be helpful to know the other person's reasons or motivation for starting or pursuing a conflict. While this may not always seem rational, it's because they are motivated by their own reasoning, not yours.

Stages of Conflict

Depending upon the individuals and issues involved, conflicts can go through a series of stages. It can be helpful to be aware of these stages and how they work to determine the best approach for resolution.

1. Pre-conflict. This is the situation before the conflict is noticed when everything is normal. Conflicts can arise very quickly over a single issue or they can build more slowly over time. Since conflicts can begin without our being aware of them, it can be helpful to check our perceptions and expectations from time to time to see if everything is all right. By talking to others, asking questions, and verifying our perceptions and expectations we can conduct a kind of relational preventative maintenance to reduce the potential of a conflict occurring.

2. Conflict escalation. At some point things go from being normal to not being normal. We may have a feeling that there is a problem, but can't be sure what it is. There may be a growing dissatisfaction, disagreement, or frustration that can turn into a conflict. If we have a problem, we should confront it, so something can be done about it. This is the best time to resolve things before they get out of hand. However, all too often it goes ignored or it escalates.

3. Conflict stabilization. At this stage everyone involved knows a conflict exists. As soon as you are aware of it, it's helpful to identify the source and the issues involved. It's helpful not to escalate a conflict, but rather to isolate it by determining its depth and breadth. It's easy for a conflict to spread, so try to limit its intensity because one conflict can cause others making things more difficult to resolve. Once these are determined, it should be easier to develop an approach to reaching a resolution. The more the people involved are motivated to resolve it, the more likely they are to come to a resolution.

4. Conflict resolution. This stage can be reached quickly or it can take some time depending upon how willing everyone is to resolve it. Resolution begins with determining the nature of the conflict and options to resolve it. Each person should be open to compromising to find a resolution. We have a personal investment in our position, so getting anything other than what we want can hurt our self-concept.

In order to avoid this, it's helpful to look at the issues without getting personal by discussing them objectively. Have everyone express their position verbally because some conflicts arise out of a need to be heard and acknowledged by others. Decision making and problem solving approaches earlier in this book can help.

5. Post conflict. Just because a resolution is reached does not necessarily mean that the conflict is over. There are often things that need to be done as part of a resolution. The solution should be properly implemented, so the conflict does not reoccur. We can improve our communicating skills by evaluating what went well and what could be done better in the future.

Approaches to Conflict

Think about your past conflicts. There were probably times you felt good about the outcome and other times it didn't go very well. How you approached conflict likely affected how you feel about it.

There is no one best way to handle conflict, so having options can help. These approaches give you options, but only you can determine what works best for you. Some types of responses include direct, indirect, and confrontational approaches.

Some of these approaches are more effective than others. Some are not recommended, but are included because they are often used, so it is helpful to be aware of them.

Approaches that resolve conflict.

• Accommodating. We accommodate others when we value our relationship with them or if someone has a higher status or more power than us, like our boss. People accommodate others when they do not want to deal with them, they feel the conflict is not worth the time and effort, they may be afraid of them, or they feel they won't get what they want. While this may not achieve your desired outcome, it can be a way to cut your losses and end the issue. You can benefit because the conflict is over and you no longer have the stress or tension associated with it.

• Cooperation. When people cooperate they work together to find a resolution. They put aside their individual needs and focus on the outcome. This approach works best when the individuals involved want to maintain a cordial relationship.

• Consensus. A conflict can be more easily resolved when everyone agrees on a solution. This approach encourages everyone to work out a solution that they can support. It works when there is pressure for everyone to agree because no one would not want to be perceived as going against the others.

• Compromise. This is when everybody gives up something they want in order to reach a resolution. This word can have a negative connotation because it gives the impression that you are giving up your values or something you want to have.

• Voting. When other methods don't work, the last resort may be to take a vote. While voting is the most democratic means of resolving conflict, it can be the least satisfactory because it can create friction between people who vote against each other.

• Cooling off period. Some conflicts create an emotional intensity that needs to be reduced before it can be addressed. In these circumstances it can be helpful to have a cooling off period to reduce the emotional intensity, so that everyone can look at things more objectively later.

Approaches that avoid conflict.

We utilize approaches to avoid conflict when we do not want to directly address a conflict. While these are generally not good approaches, it's helpful to be aware of them because they are often used.

• Avoidance. While avoidance is not an effective approach, there are some situations when it works. It is used when there is little to gain or the cost of conflict is too great. Sometimes people use conflict for intimidation, harassment, or manipulation, so avoiding them may be the best approach. It can be used when a conflict could damage a relationship or there is little chance of a positive resolution.

• Doing nothing. This is a common approach. If the conflict is not serious, it may eventually die out over time as people lose interest in it. However, doing nothing can give the perception of not caring, which can potentially make things worse. Doing nothing is different than avoidance because avoidance involves taking action to get out of the way of the other person.

• Denial. People may deny that a conflict exists or that there is a problem. They may do this hoping it will go away. They may even act sympathetic. If they do admit there's a problem, they do nothing to help resolve it.

• Ignore. When we want to discuss the conflict, others may change the subject or refuse to talk about it. They may feel that if they do not talk about it then it doesn't exist, so they don't have to deal with it.

• Apathetic. There are times when people cause conflicts and don't seem to care about the consequences. They may be fearful of the outcome or overwhelmed by having to deal with too many problems, so they act like they don't care.

• Delaying. Putting something off is a common tactic to avoid conflict. People might say they want to fix things, but keep delaying doing anything about it. They put things off in hopes the other person gets tired or forgets about it. They may feel that the longer it drags out, the less likely the other person will want to resolve it.

• Confidence. People may not resolve a conflict because they lack confidence, skills, or awareness of their options. They may feel that it is easier just to go along with everyone else. They may feel it's better to keep the peace than to fight.

• Abandonment. Sometimes people don't want anything to do with the conflict, so they dump it on someone else or just walk away. This can happen when someone feels overwhelmed or that they have no chance of getting what they want.

• Humor. Humor is used as a way to defuse tension or avoid taking responsibility. In some conflicts people use humor to make fun of or joke about someone as a way of communicating their problems or conflicts.

• Placating. The purpose of this approach is to please the other person instead of finding an equitable resolution. It is used in conflicts when one person may have a fear of conflict, rejection, or of the other person. They might do this if they feel they don't have a good case, the other person is more powerful, or they want something else in return later.

• Obligation. This involves motivating others to do something out of a sense of duty or loyalty. They may have done someone a favor and now want something in return.

• Emotion. People use emotional appeals to persuade others to do what they want. A common approach is using guilt to make the other person feel that they are somehow responsible for the problem.

• Calculating. This is the opposite of the emotional approach because it is characterized by the lack of emotion. Calculating treats conflict as a game and people as pawns, where the objective is to vanquish the opponent to win.

• Blaming. Instead of looking to resolve the conflict, one person blames the other for the problem to shift the responsibility off them on to someone else.

• Martyrdom. This is the opposite of blaming. It is a form of self sacrifice where one person takes responsibility for the conflict and is willing to pay the price. They may portray themselves as unjustly persecuted to gain sympathy by playing on people's good nature.

• Sufficing. This is when people do something easy that suffices for working out a real solution. They take the easiest solution whether it works or not. While this is a poor way to resolve conflict, it is done surprisingly often.

• Bargaining. This approach treats conflict like deal making where people trade one concession for another. They may ask for things they don't want, so that they can give them up creating the illusion of making concessions.

• Distracting. This involves creating another problem or crisis to divert attention away from the real conflict. If another situation is perceived as worse, people will forget about the conflict because they have only so much time and energy.

• Repetition. Some people approach conflict by repeating the same thing over and over until the other person gives up or other people start to believe them. When something is repeated over and over, it can take on a validity of its own whether it is true or not.

• Coexisting. This is when both parties acknowledge the conflict, but it is not resolved. They agreed to do different things for a period of time to see how it goes. This approach can be used when an agreement cannot be reached.

• Subversive. This happens when a conflict has been resolved, but one party refuses to accept that they lost, so they keep on pressing their case to try to get their way or undermine the outcome. If they can't win on their merit they will try to attack their opponent personally, and if that fails they attack the process. Versions of this approach include using protests, boycotts, harassment, recalls, or litigation.

• Covert. Instead of telling the other person there is a problem, they go behind their back and tell others. They may want to gain sympathy or turn others against them. The other person does not know there is a problem and so can't do anything about it, so others might think they don't care.

Approaches that intensify conflict.

These are more confrontational approaches that use power, control, or manipulation to force others into a resolution. Winning can be more important than working things out. This can leave the losing party feeling defeated. While these are not good approaches to resolve conflict, it is surprising how often they are used.

People may use the following approaches because they feel they cannot win by normal means, so they try to discredit, sabotage, or hurt others. They try to pressure others to get what they want. It may be best to defuse the situation by having a cooling off period, clarifying the issues, or avoiding them if possible.

• Competition. Instead of trying to reach a satisfactory resolution, some people see conflict as a competition they must win. They are out to get what they want regardless of the cost. This can be useful when a quick decision is needed like in a crisis, however, it can do more damage or escalate the conflict.

• Ambushing. This is a deceptive approach where one person listens to the other, but instead resolving the conflict they try to get the other person to say or do something that can be used against them. So, be careful what you tell them.

• Leverage. This approach seeks to deny someone something they need or want unless the other person gets their way. Changing what you want can take it away.

• Confrontation. This approach uses hostility to intimidate others to get their way. People may be confrontational because they have a weak case or are afraid of losing something. Backing away for a while can help to reduce the intensity.

• Control. Some people view conflict as a challenge to their authority, so they feel they need to exert control over others to win. If they compromise on one thing they may be forced to compromise on everything.

• Manipulation. This approach forces or tricks others to support them. Manipulation can include using sympathy, guilt, or fear. Rewards and punishments can be used to coerce others to do what they want.

• Blackmail. This is a specific form of manipulation that uses threats of retaliation to get the other person to do what they want. It can involve threats to reveal potentially embarrassing information. It can be withholding of something of value like fulfillment of needs and wants. It can be preventing them from doing something or achieving a desired outcome.

• Intimidation. This is motivating others to do something by harassing, belittling, or threatening them. This creates fear in their mind, so they do what others want.

• Aggression. In resolving conflict, aggressiveness can be anything from being obsessive to physically threatening. This can make the other person feel humiliated, embarrassed, or fearful of retaliation.

• Anger. Conflict can become emotionally charged leading to verbal aggressiveness. People may get angry not only to vent their emotions, but also to scare others to motivate them into doing what they want. Under these circumstances the best approach may be to stop and get away from the other person until things cool off.

• Self righteousness. Some people feel that they are always right about everything all the time. When faced with conflict, they may see it as a personal attack because they think they are concerned with everyone else's welfare.

• Force. Some conflicts are resolved by sheer force. Force can be mental, emotional, even physical. This approach is utilized when people think they can use power to control others to give up their position, so they can get what they want.

• Shutting out. This is a more passive means of using force when one person tries to get their way by refusing to listen to others. They get their way by being closed off, effectively shutting out the other person preventing them from doing anything.

• External forces. Some people use forces outside of themselves to justify their actions or to motivate others to give in to what they want. They may take the moral high ground, call on spiritual or religious doctrine, or claim they are doing a higher power's work so they can get their way.

• Panic. This is creating a false sense of urgency so others believe the conflict has to be resolved immediately to avert a disaster. This approach can force people to make quick decisions before they have the time to think things through. If they had more time they probably wouldn't go along. This approach can be used to manipulate others when they don't have a strong argument.

Approaches that create unnecessary conflict.

There are some instances when people start a conflict just for the sake of having one. Under these circumstances there is little hope of resolution, so it's best to stay away from them.

• Entertainment. Some people might create conflict for fun, entertainment, or excitement. They may have a need for power or control. These conflicts often have little substance, so there is no real solution. If someone is behaving like this, you might let them know how others perceive them.

• Acknowledgment. This can happen with children or adolescents who may provoke conflicts to get people to notice them or to assert their independence. There may be other ways to meet these needs other than through conflict. Acknowledging them or giving them more independence can help to reduce these conflicts.

• Conflict conflicts. Some people love a good fight, so they create conflicts to feel important or bolster their self-concept. They might use them as a means to prove that they are right, knowledgeable, or accomplished. Resolving these conflicts can be difficult because they never give up. The best approach is to avoid them.

Approaches to formally resolve conflict.

When other approaches fail or when directly communicating with the other party is not feasible, formal third party approaches can help facilitate a resolution. These approaches are a good alternative when our abilities, skills, or resources are not capable of reaching a satisfactory solution.

• Third party approaches. This approach uses intermediaries to reach a resolution. This can be useful in circumstances when direct contact with the other party is not effective. This can be a useful approach when there is emotional intensity or hostility between the parties. It can be used if there is a history of conflict or if the parties are not able to meet face to face.

• Rules approach. This approach uses written rules to resolve a conflict. It can be used when a solution needs to be impartial or objective. To reach a solution, everyone needs to agree on what rules apply and how to apply them. This approach is often used in sports or legal conflicts by using rules and laws for resolution.

• Formal approaches. These approaches to conflict resolution include arbitration, negotiation, mediation, and litigation. They often utilize outside experts who have a specific skill to help resolve the conflict like an attorney or mediator.

Conflict Resolution Skills

Conflict resolution means bringing a conflict to an end.
It does not necessarily mean that it is resolved
the way you want it to be resolved.

You may get what you want, only part of what you want, or nothing at all. Sometimes it's better to have it over and done with by cutting your losses and ending the conflict.

Even if you don't get what you want, there can be benefits by no longer having to deal with the tension, stress, and frustration that can accompany a conflict.

When it's over you can relax and forget about it. This can free up your time and energy to use on more fun and productive activities.

No one wins every conflict, but by having a variety of approaches and using communicating skills effectively, you can feel better about how you approached a conflict regardless of the outcome.

The following are some approaches for conflict resolution.

• Determine what the conflict is actually about. There are times when people get into disagreements about something only to realize that they are both arguing the same position or about nothing substantial at all.

• Determine the scope of the issues. Then set boundaries to limit what is going to be discussed. This keeps the conflict from escalating.

• Determine if the conflict is worth spending your time and energy on before going any further because some conflicts are not worth the trouble.

• Listen to what the other person is saying to avoid misunderstandings that can cause unnecessary conflict. Listening to what they have to say does not mean that you have to accept their position or agree with it. Doing this can give you more information to understand the issues and the motivation for their behavior.

If you want others to listen to you, you must be willing to listen to them. They may know something you don't, so you might learn something. By understanding their position you are better able to resolve the situation. All too often people assume they know the other person's position and end up fighting about nothing at all.

• Ask the other person questions to get more information. This can divert their attention by getting them to talk. They may be taken off guard by this response, so they might not know how to respond. Doing this can help to avoid misunderstandings that could potentially make a conflict worse.

• Reduce uncertainty by being prepared, so you can stay calm and not retaliate or escalate the conflict. It takes self control to stay calm in high pressure situations. By being prepared you can develop skills that will help you when you need it.

• Have a plan. Sometimes people put others on the spot because that's how they think they will get what they want. They may try to take the other person by surprise to get their way. So, have a plan for conflict and be prepared or you may react out of habit or emotion escalating the conflict.

• Look for shared meaning by finding something you have in common with the other person. This can be helpful because coming to a resolution often begins by finding common ground.

• Be aware of what others are saying and how you are coming across to them. Be aware of how you express emotions to avoid saying something you might regret later.

• Avoid humor, while it can lighten the tension, it can give the impression you are not serious about the issue. Avoid making assumptions or jumping to conclusions about the other person.

• Put yourself in the other person's position to see the situation from their perspective. You do not have to agree with them, but it can help you to better understand them.

• Show respect and treat others the way you want to be treated. It doesn't hurt to be polite and courteous to others. Doing this can help because finding a resolution is not just up to you, it's also up to them.

• Use the law of investing to encourage everyone to find a resolution, so they do not lose what they have already invested in the process.

• Be a leader. Look for potential solutions and offer a way to reach a resolution. If you don't take an active role, you may find yourself being shut out or pushed into doing things that you do not want to do.

• Encourage others by acknowledging their position. This shows that you have listened to them and understand their position. This does not mean that you necessarily agree with them. Avoiding others or ignoring what they have to say can communicate that you do not care about them potentially making them more determined to get their way.

By understanding the other person's position, you can appeal to their sense of fairness and what is in your mutual best interest. People can be more likely to reach a mutually accepted resolution if they feel that you are motivated out of concern for them as well as yourself.

• Consider how your relationship may be affected by the conflict because some conflicts could damage a relationship. Consider what you will gain compared to what you may lose. Ask yourself, is it more important to win the argument or preserve the relationship?

It can be more helpful to work with the other person to develop a means to resolve the conflict while supporting the relationship. A supportive relationship should be able to withstand conflict without damaging it.

• Consider your desired outcome. If someone confronts you they may expect you to react, so they will have likely prepared for you to defend yourself. If you don't get defensive, you can reduce the emotional intensity because they may not be expecting it. Consider your desired outcome, is it to escalate or resolve the conflict?

It has been said, choose your battles wisely. We do not have the resources to fight every fight. Some things are worth fighting for and others are not. You don't want to take on battles that could be costly with little chance of success. There should be no dishonor in a gracious retreat.

• Avoid explaining yourself. When someone confronts us there is a natural tendency to explain ourselves. This can be seen as being defensive or an admission of guilt. It gives others more information, which is not in your best interest.

In more serious situations, do not give information to anyone in authority or who may be able to use that information against you later. Exercise your right to remain silent until you understand the situation and have legal counsel or advice.

Your desired outcome should be to get more information from them because if you are attacked or accused of something, you should know what it is and why. The more information you can get, the better your chances are of reaching a resolution.

• Avoid stating opinion as fact, instead express them as opinions or feelings. For instance, instead of saying, "You were wrong" you might say something like, "I had a feeling that was wrong." Feelings cannot be proven to be right or wrong because they are your own. Use descriptive rather than judgmental language. Rather than calling something bad use specific examples.

• Avoid getting dragged into other people's problems. Sometimes we get drawn into a conflict we should avoid. Just because someone else has a conflict does not mean you have to join in too. We may get involved in a conflict and then discover more serious underlying problems.

If things aren't working out, by using communicating skills you can at least feel that you have tried everything possible. When it comes to conflict you have options and one is to walk away.

People don't always confront others in private, they can verbally attack others in places where other people are around. Stop to consider what those other people might say about you and what happened because you do not want to be perceived as being the aggressor.

Do not become defensive or attack them back, instead express your concern. Doing this makes you look confident and sympathetic in front of others. If you attack an aggressor, regardless what they did to you, people are likely to sympathize with them because you retaliated, even though you had every right to do so.

In a conflict or when put on the spot, don't feel obliged to explain yourself.

Two skills that can help resolve a conflict are competence and confidence. Competence is your ability to communicate with others, having an awareness of the situation, and options for resolving a conflict. It is having an awareness of your skills and the ability to use them effectively.

Confidence is having faith in yourself and your abilities. It is the ability to communicate effectively to help achieve your desired outcome. In a conflict, people are more likely to be receptive to someone who shows competence because they seem knowledgeable. People are likely to be persuaded by someone who is confident, because their demeanor helps to reduce uncertainty.

A Process for Resolving Conflict

It would be great if conflict resolution was as simple as sitting down with someone to talk it over. There are some situations when it can be helpful to have an organized process to find a solution. By using an organized process to work through conflict, it can be resolved more effectively.

The following approach provides you with options to resolve conflict.

1. Formal or informal. When first faced with a conflict, there is a natural tendency to respond impulsively in the moment. Instead, have an organized process to work out the conflict. It should be appropriate for the circumstances and the people involved. For example, conflict between family members could be handled informally around the kitchen table. A work relationship might utilize a more formal process in an office or conference room.

2. Agree on the rules. If there are no rules about how to resolve the conflict, it's easy for things to break down into a free for all where nothing gets done. Agreeing on a few rules can make the process run much smoother. For example, some rules can include no derogatory or inflammatory statements or interrupting others.

3. Agree to meet. Having a meeting may sound overly formal, but it's important to get everyone together, so they can have their say.

4. Agree on a time to meet that everyone can get together. Enough time should be set aside so everyone can be heard. There should be an ending time to discourage dragging things out. If the issue cannot be resolved, additional time can be set up.

5. Agree on a place to meet. It should be comfortable so everyone can relax and focus on the issues, but not so comfortable that they will want to stay for a long time. It should be free from distractions and appropriate to the people involved like a home, office, or a neutral location. It should protect everyone's privacy away from others who could listen in.

6. Agree on an agenda. Even informal meetings should have an agenda so the discussion stays on track. An agenda is a listing of the items to be discussed in chronological order, along with the time allotted for each. It's easy to go off on a tangent, so having an agenda keeps everyone on track.

7. Agree on the issues. Everyone may agree there is conflict, but they may not agree what the conflict is about. Agreement helps to avoid wasting time on unimportant things. Clearly establishing the limits and scope of the discussion can help everyone stay focused. This keeps everyone from arguing about unimportant things that can hurt the process and prevent a resolution.

Conducting the meeting.

Having a meeting can help reach a resolution. It lets everyone say what's on their mind. Sometimes all people really want is to be heard and acknowledged.

These are things to do during the meeting.

1. Start with a positive atmosphere to reduce tension so people can relax and work together. Meet in a place that's comfortable and free of distractions. You might have refreshments, like water or coffee to make them feel welcome.

2. Introductions. It can be helpful for everyone to get to know each other, if they don't already. Have each person introduce themselves. Using self-disclosure can reduce uncertainty to help find common ground to reach a resolution.

3. Describe the process. It can be helpful to quickly review the agenda so everyone has realistic expectations of what the meeting should accomplish.

4. Presenting positions. Give each person a few minutes to present their position without interruption. This may be the first time they have all heard each other. It gets everything out in the open, clarifies the issues, and helps keep things on track.

5. Find common ground. At this point there should be some common ground. In order to reach a resolution, start with things everyone already agrees upon, and then work on areas of disagreement. This can provide some momentum toward reaching a solution by starting with agreement instead of disagreement.

6. Reach a solution. Go around the room and have each person contribute their best idea to make a list of possible solutions. Then have them choose the best one or two. The section on decision making has several options that can help. Some include compromise, collaboration, or consensus. If one doesn't work, try another.

7. When an agreement is reached, write it down and give everyone a copy because later people may have different recollections of what was decided. Evaluate the effectiveness of the solution including what worked and what could be improved.

Negotiation

There are times when a more formal or structured process is needed to reach a resolution. Negotiation is a more structured method of conflict resolution or decision making.

Negotiation often includes a written agreement or contract that sets out the terms of the resolution. It is used when making financial commitments like buying a car or house. It can set out the terms of employment when being hired for a job. If the agreement is legally binding, it's best to get professional advice before signing it.

When we buy something that costs a lot of money we generally don't just walk in and pay for it. Instead we negotiate the price, financing, and other terms that are set out in a written agreement. An employment contract often includes salary, length of employment, duties, and responsibilities. It is helpful to know how to negotiate because practically everyone will do it at some point.

Negotiation is about value and value is often determined by perception.

Negotiation strategies involve shaping perceptions and expectations. In negotiation, each party gives up something to get what they want.

This can motivate people to initially ask for more than they really want. Then they can give up something they asked for knowing that they don't really want it.

You usually negotiate for yourself when you make purchases like a car or apply for a job. However, the more money that's involved, the more specialized the field, and the more complicated the issues, the more it is in your best interest to utilize a professional negotiator. For example, we use a real estate agent when buying a house or an agent or attorney when negotiating a contract.

To find the most effective approach determine your desired outcome, but have reasonable expectations about what you want because there's only so much the other party can do.

Avoid making negotiations personal. Show the other party respect and consideration regardless of what they might say or do. It helps to be perceived as being fair, open minded, calm, professional, and rational.

If you are negotiating with someone you know, put the relationship ahead of the negotiation. You don't want to be perceived as being inconsiderate with someone whose friendship you value. People might say, "It's just business," but it's not, it's always personal.

Formal negotiations are often conducted by a designated leader. However, when you negotiate on your own, like when buying a car, you should take the lead.

Determine your desired outcome and do your homework, so that you know as much information as you can about what you want.

Keep the negotiation on track. Do not let the other person push you into something you do not want to do. The other person should give you time to think things over.

They should let you show any written agreement to someone else like an attorney. If they don't or it doesn't seem right, walk away.

Know you limits ahead of time and stay within them.
If something doesn't seem right, don't be afraid to walk away.

The negotiation process.

Negotiation begins by presenting an offer. Initially, neither person offers what they actually want. If they did, it would not be a negotiation. If there are terms to the agreement, these are also presented.

When money is involved, a buyer typically starts lower than they want to pay and a seller starts higher than they are willing to sell. This gives them room to negotiate until they find a price in the middle they can both agree on.

Each person may ask for things they don't want or more than they want, so they can have room to negotiate and can make concessions. They may use some items as a diversion to draw attention away from what they really want.

This creates a perception that they have compromised because negotiation is about giving something up in order to gain something better.

Negotiation can determine how important each item is to the other by testing their willingness to keep it in the final agreement.

By utilizing communicating skills, you can better understand why some things just don't work out. It's better to know that you tried then to wonder what went wrong thinking that there was something else you could have done.

In negotiating it's helpful to keep these things in mind.
- As much as we do things to keep control of a situation, the only thing that we can really control is ourselves.
- Regardless of whatever is happening around you stay in control.
- Decide what you are willing to do and not do be you begin.
- Have boundaries and stick to them.
- Do not let others manipulate or maneuver you.
- Stay focused on your desired outcome.
- Avoid escalating a situation by saying something in the heat of the moment you might regret later.

Options for effective negotiation and conflict resolution.

• Use the law of uncertainty. Conflict can increase uncertainty because people do not know what to expect. Reaching a resolution lets people know what to expect, which can reduce tension and uncertainty increasing stability.

• Use the law of shared meaning. Listen to find common values or interests that can encourage a resolution. Use appropriate self-disclosure to build trust. Negotiations need not be only task oriented. Having some social time can help relieve tension and help people to work together.

• Use the law of investing. Point out that everyone has invested their time and energy in the process. If a resolution isn't reached they could lose that investment, so it is in their best interest to find some agreement. There is usually some area that everyone can agree on, which can be a first step toward reaching a broader solution.

• Consider the needs, wants, perceptions, and expectations of others. People may not be comfortable talking about their needs and wants, so it's helpful to know if they are not being met.

• Understand their expectations for reaching resolution including those they have of themselves and others. Take some time to talk about how well their perceptions are meeting their expectations.

• Consider the desired outcomes of others and what they are able to do. Consider your own desired outcomes including not just what you want to gain, but what you are willing to do. Know your limits and stick to them.

This process can be time and energy consuming leaving people feeling tired or frustrated. When people get tired, emotions and tensions may run high hindering progress.

Taking a break can reduce stress and tension. It lets everyone get away from the situation so that they can recuperate. Breaks can include coffee, lunch, or adjourning for the evening if necessary.

Taking a break can be helpful because it can be better to take a break when things are not going well than to continue. If you feel that you are being pressured or manipulated, ask to take a break to relieve the pressure.

If nothing seems to be working remember that not everything can be resolved. You can never know everything there is to know about others and what they are able to do. They may not be able to come to an agreement for a variety of reasons that have nothing to do with you.

Chapter 17
Be Better Prepared in a Crisis

Crisis is a natural part of life and we all experience some kind of crisis in our lives. What constitutes a crisis depends upon who is involved, our perceptions and expectations, and our preparation and training to handle it.

What can be a crisis for one person may be another day at work for someone else. For example, emergency responders like police, firefighters, and paramedics respond to crisis situations because they are prepared to respond. The better we are prepared, the less likely we are to perceive something as a crisis.

These are some characteristics of a crisis.

• Crisis poses a threat to stability that increases uncertainty. A crisis can threaten basic needs and wants like our health or safety. A crisis can be the loss of something we have, like the loss of a house in a natural disaster or the loss of a spouse in a divorce. We may experience many different kinds of crisis such as personal, relational, financial, emotional, spiritual, and medical.

• Crisis demands a response. We need to make decisions and take action to protect ourselves, our family, our safety, or our security. We may experience events outside of our ability to cope with them. So, we may need new resources and ways of doing things to respond.

• Crisis can hurt our well-being, state of mind, health, or relationships. It can bring out the best and worst in people. Some rise to the challenge while others might try to avoid it or attribute blame.

• Crisis has time limits. It can last for a while, then it passes. However, its effects may last much longer, even a lifetime. There is often a limited amount of time to respond creating urgency and pressure to take action.

• Crisis creates new norms. When a crisis occurs it increases stress beyond what we can handle, so we need support and new ways of doing things. After a crisis, we might keep some of these new ways, so that we can deal with crisis more effectively in the future.

• Crisis means mobilizing resources. Our resources can be quickly overwhelmed, so we have to find additional resources. We look to groups like our family, friends, church, community, or the government for help to provide them.

• Crisis is a sudden and extreme increase in uncertainty motivating us to take immediate action. It can undermine our feelings of safety and security making the future less certain and predictable. It can make us look for new ways of doing things. It can affect our lives long after the crisis has passed.

Reduce the uncertainty crisis creates by being prepared and planning ahead.

However, we often don't do it because we think a crisis will never happen to us, so we may not prepare for it until after we have experienced one.

Phases of Crisis

Crisis can be easier to cope with if approached as a series of phases.

1. The law of uncertainty phase. A crisis can begin with a rapid and dramatic increase in uncertainty undermining our stability and security. It overwhelms our resources and methods of problem solving. There is often a limited amount of time to respond and the longer it takes, the more serious the consequences may be.

What constitutes a crisis may be difficult to define, but everyone involved knows when one happens. What makes a crisis depends on how we perceive and interpret events based upon our past experiences and skills.

What constitutes a crisis for one person may not for others. Crisis creates feelings of anxiety, anger, or fear because we do not know what to do or what will happen.

2. The law of shared meaning phase. When everyone involved is aware of the crisis, they begin communicating about it. They invest what is happening with shared meaning. The need to communicate dramatically increases to the point where it may overwhelm the ability of existing communicating networks to handle it.

When people communicate, they characterize the crisis in terms that are negative or positive. How people communicate about the crisis in its early stages can affect their perception of what is happening to them shaping their expectations. This can motivate their behavior, with tangible consequences affecting how successful the outcome will be.

In a crisis we might get information from family, friends, the media, experts, public officials, or professionals who are trained to handle a crisis. The nature of this information can change the emotional intensity of the situation.

Negative messages can create the perception that things are going badly causing people to become apprehensive or even panic. This can diminish their ability to react to their circumstances.

Negative messages can increase uncertainty undermining people's confidence making them less likely to do what is necessary in a crisis, which could make the situation worse.

Communicating positive messages can help give people confidence to do what is necessary in a crisis. If people have the perception that the crisis is something they can handle, they may expect things to work out giving them the confidence to handle them more effectively.

3. The law of investing phase. A crisis is an overwhelming increase in uncertainty that motivates people to take action to return to a normal, stable state. Eventually the level of uncertainty reaches a peak or turning point where it begins to subside either naturally or through the efforts of people to resolve it.

Negative messages should be diminishing and more positive messages should be increasing as people focus their attention from the crisis itself to what needs to be done afterwards. The emotional intensity should drop as people begin to feel a sense of relief that the worst is over.

In this phase, we seek to restore the previous state of normality or if that's not possible establish a new state of normality or stability. Because a crisis overwhelms old norms or ways of doing things, we can be motivated to find new ways of doing things to resolve the crisis.

One of the positive aspects of crisis is that it gets people to think about things that are familiar to them in new ways. New norms that were effective in resolving the crisis might be kept. We can learn from our experience to take a bad thing and turn it around to make it better. Even in bad situations, it can be helpful to look for the good things that we can benefit from.

It can take some time to come to terms with the crisis. We may need time to think about and process our experiences because some things are difficult to assimilate. This works like the perception process where we select, organize, and interpret the information we perceive to fit it in with what we already know, so it can be useful to us.

We do this to fit present reality in with our perceptions of past experiences. The degree to which we are able to process the information determines how well adjusted we are with the experience.

4. After a crisis. How we feel after a crisis can have a significant affect on our self-concept. If we feel things went as well as they could, it can improve our self-concept making us feel confident about our abilities. If we feel that things could have gone better, it can hurt our self-concept. By evaluating our skills, we can be better prepared for what may happen in the future.

Once uncertainty has been reduced we may try to establish a stable set of norms. However, things may not return to how they were before, but instead there will be a new state of stability or normality. The degree of difference can be determined by the severity of the crisis and how much it forced us to make changes.

In a crisis, we can learn new ways of doing things, making decisions, obtaining information, using resources, and making connections with others for support. This can motivate us to make changes we may have wanted to make, but haven't.

If a crisis passes quickly people are more likely to return to norms like they had before the crisis because they are familiar. If a crisis drags on, they are more likely to get accustomed to the changes crisis brings. They are less likely to return to the norms they had before the crisis. Eventually, they may become accustomed to the new norms.

Crisis Preparation

When it comes to crisis the old adage, be prepared still applies. Preparation and training helps to reduce uncertainty and improve effectiveness in a crisis. It can help to develop options to respond to potential sources of crisis.

In order to be better prepared for a crisis, it can be helpful to conduct a crisis assessment and develop a plan. A plan can reduce uncertainty and be a source of confidence in a crisis. Anticipating a crisis can be helpful to avoid ones that can be avoided and mitigate the effects of those that are inevitable.

Moments for avoiding a crisis, as well as unintended or undesired outcomes.

1. Moment of no return. This is when a course of action can't be reversed or stopped. For example, it is when the ship can no longer change course in time to avoid hitting the iceberg.

2. Moment of realization. This is when people know what is going to happen. For example, it is when the crew realizes the ship will hit the iceberg.

It is important which moment comes first. If the moment of no return happens first, the ship will hit the iceberg and be lost. If the moment of realization happens first, the ship can change course to avoid the iceberg and will be saved. Knowing this can help to avoid potential crises, which is why awareness is so important.

Options for developing a crisis plan.

1. What crisis might happen? Identify any potential crisis that might happen to you. Determine the sources of the crisis and your desired outcomes during and after the crisis.

2. What will you need? Identify the resources you will need and gather them together, including water, food, clothing, and money. Have any items you may need ready to go at a moments notice. Identify outside resources that you might need like emergency responders. Consider how much time you will need to get to a place of safety or to get help.

3. What will you do? Create a plan of action. Determine what needs attention now, what can wait, and what is out of your control. For example, a medical crisis needs attention now, a financial crisis might wait, and in a natural disaster all you may be able to do is wait until it passes.

Determine what things you can do yourself and which ones need support from others. Have an alternative plan as well just in case the first plan cannot be implemented.

4. Rehearse. Test the plan by practicing it so you know what to do under actual circumstances. Doing this can help you to feel more confident when it comes to implementing the plan because it will feel more familiar.

5. Communicate. Think about how you will get information. You may not be able to depend on telephone service, so consider other ways to communicate with others. Keep things positive and concentrate on what can be done to keep calm and focused. Avoid negative messages that can scare people increasing anxiety or uncertainty.

6. Implement. If it's necessary to implement a crisis plan, start with the scope and nature of the crisis to avoid overreacting. By knowing exactly what is involved, you can focus on the things that need to be done now and put off less pressing things until you have more time.

The best time to plan for a crisis is now, before
something happens because once it does, it's too late to plan ahead.

We have a tendency to put off doing this because these things happen to other people. So, having a plan gives you options to select the best one to fit your situation.

We learn how to handle a crisis from our experiences, but it can be helpful to talk about your experiences with others to gain more insight and information.

Chapter 18
Be Better-Looking by Being Healthy

It's been said that, it's what's on the inside that counts. While this generally means who we are as a person, it also pertains to our health and well-being.

Our health affects our behavior and appearance. When we feel good we look good because we have a better self-concept, so we act confident. While we all want to have good health, our well-being is often subject to uncertainty.

We can reduce uncertainty about our health by having effective communicating skills to gain information, so we can better understand our health care options to make good decisions.

Our health can benefit when we know how to;
* Have accurate perceptions and realistic expectations.
* Develop a positive self-concept.
* Create and maintain positive relationships.
* Communicate with family members.
* Work effectively in groups.
* Communicate with medical professionals.
* Do research using credible sources.
* Manage stress and emotions like anger.
* Work through conflicts.
* Be prepared for a crisis.
* Reduce uncertainty.

Understanding how the laws of uncertainty, shared meaning, and investing work can help to diagnose and treat physical and mental health issues. In diagnosing illness we look for the cause or symptoms in order to find a treatment. However, there could be a deeper, underlying cause.

For instance, someone may have a sleep or digestive disorder that is caused by stress or anxiety. Their mental state may be manifesting itself in a physical illness caused by uncertainty. So, in diagnosing medical problems, it can be helpful to look at how uncertainty could be affecting them.

Our mental state can affect our physical state. Many of the emotions we feel like anxiety, fear, and anger can have health consequences. Increased uncertainty can lead to stress, anxiety, and depression.

If we are having difficulties in our relationships, it could hurt our confidence and self-concept. These things can affect our health because psychological perceptions can have physical consequences.

Uncertainty has the potential to be an underlying source of medical and psychological conditions because social reality can create physical reality.

Our relationships can also affect our health. If we have a good communicating network and support system, it can improve our confidence and self-concept, which can help us feel better. When we feel good, we have better nonverbal body language including improved posture, bearing, and even more positive facial expressions like eye contact and smiling. This can make us better-looking to others and if we receive positive feedback, it can bolster our self-confidence.

If we share little meaning with others, we might feel alone, withdrawn, or depressed. We may have negative body language with diminished posture, bearing, eye contact, or facial expressions. This may be seen as a lack of confidence, so feedback can be more negative hurting our self-confidence.

We invest in relationships because they can make us feel good about ourselves bolstering our self-concept, which can improve our health. We can also invest in ourselves, which includes both our physical and mental well-being. Communicating effectively can help us to have positive relationships. When we share meaning with others it can make us feel needed and appreciated. This helps provide us with support and nurturing.

Our perceptions and expectations can have an affect on our health. When our perceptions are accurate and our expectations are reasonable, we can feel good. If our perceptions are not meeting our expectations it can make us feel sad, depressed, or even angry, which can affect our mental as well as physical health. Feelings can motivate us to eat, drink, or smoke to feel better even though it is harmful.

Good health is one of our most important needs and we want to feel good. However, the need to be healthy and wanting to feel good can be one of the most challenging set of conflicting needs and wants we have.

We enjoy eating food that tastes good, but we also need to eat healthy. We need to exercise, but we like to relax. It can be difficult to find the right balance between conflicting needs and wants, so having awareness and options can help.

We take care of our possessions like our car or our house, but it's all to easy to neglect taking care of ourselves. By developing communicating skills, we can gain many health benefits. We can improve the quality of our health by reducing uncertainty, to lower blood pressure, reduce hypertension, and the risk of heart disease.

Improving awareness can help us to know more about our health because everyone will likely face health issues at sometime in their life. We can have more options to be better prepared to find the best solutions for good health to improve our quality of life.

Conclusion

There are times when we say something that makes us wonder why we said it. There are times we behave in ways that make us wonder if we really know who we are. We may feel tension or frustration and not really know why.

By understanding how communicating works,
* We can better understand the forces that affect what we say and do.
* We can better understand why we feel the way we do.
* We can better understand our needs and wants, and what motivates us.
* We can make informed choices to do something about these things, rather than letting uncertainty control us.
* And we can simplify our life to focus on what is important, to improve our quality of life.

Throughout history, most of human activity has been motivated by uncertainty. The pursuit of reducing uncertainty should have resulted in a significant decrease in the amount of uncertainty people experience. However, today it seems that more people experience greater uncertainty than ever before in history.

Society has made great advancements to reduce uncertainty, but has it also made us more vulnerable to the effects of uncertainty?

Perhaps, the more complicated our systems become, the more vulnerable they are to uncertainty. Perhaps we should be looking to encourage independence and self reliance in order to flow with uncertainty rather than trying to control it.

In an increasingly interconnected world, how do we protect ourselves from the potential affects of increasing uncertainty? While we may never fully control or even understand the nature of uncertainty one thing is certain, absolute uncertainty will be a part of our lives now and in the future.

www.ingramcontent.com/pod-product-compliance
Lightning Source LLC
LaVergne TN
LVHW011155080426
835508LV00007B/427